Digital Deceptions

TIME TO MAKE BETTER CHOICES

Amir Abdelzaher, PhD
Ahmed Howeedy, MD
Arfan Qureshi, MA

© Sagetree Foundation 2020
First published in July 2024 by:
Ta-Ha Publishers Ltd.
Unit 4, The Windsor Centre,
Windsor Grove,
London, SE27 9NT
United Kingdom

www.**tahapublishers.com**
support@tahapublishers.com

All rights reserved. No part of this publication may be reproduced, stored in any retrieval system, or transmitted in any form or by any means, electronic, mechanical, photocopying, recording or otherwise, without the prior written permission of the publishers.

Written by: **Dr Amir Abdelzaher, Dr Ahmed Howeedy** and **Arfan Qureshi**
Edited by: **Dr Abia Afsar-Siddiqui**
Cover Design and Typeset by: **Shakir Abdulcadir**

A catalogue record of this book is available from the British Library
ISBN: 978-1-915357-38-0 (paperback)
10 9 8 7 6 5 4 3 2 1

Printed and bound by: Mega Basim, Türkiye

Sagetree Foundation is dedicated to reviving the light and wisdom of the Prophets and sages to help seekers in the modern world navigate the confusions and darknesses that have permeated all aspects of life.

Sagetree Foundation
6278 N Federal Highway, Suite 478
Ft. Lauderdale, FL, USA 33308
www.sagetreefoundation.org

…Then give glad tidings to My Servants who listen closely to all that is said, and follow the best of it, for it is they whom God has graced with His guidance, and it is they who are truly endowed with insight.

Qur'an 39:17-18

Contents

Preface 6
Introduction 8

Perceived Benefits, Real Harms

Chapter 1 The Common Narrative: Breaking Misconceptions 13
Chapter 2 Digital Addiction: Impact on the Brain 39
Chapter 3 Privacy, Surveillance, Manipulation 53
Chapter 4 Welcome to the Age of AI 73

Time to Make Better Choices

Chapter 5 Principles of Personal Change 91
Chapter 6 Parenting in the Digital Age 119
Chapter 7 Healthy Living in the Digital Age 131
Chapter 8 The Greatest Means 137

The Road Ahead

Chapter 9 Final Thoughts 145

Preface

It's passé to call the world a global village. It is now a virtual, global village. And while some of us have accepted this, and even embraced it, as our new existential reality, we have yet to fully appreciate the significance of our newfound *suhba*.

Suhba – fellowship or, more generally, one's interactive environment – is one of the most salient factors in shaping our words, deeds, habits and belief systems. The Messenger of God ﷺ warned: an individual will take on the *deen*, the religious value system, of his or her close friend, so beware whom you befriend.

In many ways, virtual *suhba* is more impactful and perilous than physical *suhba*. Virtual *suhba* is more available and accessible. It offers a more private and personal portal (think of how difficult it was for a boy to meet a girl in the old village, without smartphones, instant messaging, voice and video chat). And it is more encompassing in its offering of anything and everything.

Yes, I should be very concerned. What is the impact on my spiritual heart (*qalb*), gifted to me to know, experience and seek the Infinite? How will this *suhba* affect my pursuit of the ultimate happiness and the deepest freedom? How will the young minds and heart entrusted to my care fare when exposed to the near irresistible?

One might suggest that there are three ways to use digital technology: *taqwa*-use, *wara'*-use, and *ihsan*-use. *Taqwa*-use is to use technology without falling into the impermissible and harmful (*haram*).

This use is obligatory. *Wara'*-use is to use technology without permissible excess. This use is not obligatory, but recommended. And *ihsan*-use is to use technology to only seek what the Divine loves. This use is not obligatory but the intent of the seeker of Divine love (*mahabba*).

Let me strive for a relationship with the digital world that is slowly and surely better and more beneficial for me and my loved ones.

May Allah bless and reward the authors of this work for a labour that comprehensively addresses a critical need of our time.

May their work guide the steps of our *suhba* with the digital world to lead to the *suhba* of the Beloved ﷺ and, through him, to the Ultimate Companion, the Real (*al-Haqq*). Ameen.

Riad Saloojee
Al-Madina's, Suhba Seminary
February 2024

Introduction

For too long, we have embraced and rationalised nearly every technological and digital "advancement" in the name of convenience, enjoyment, and productivity. We race to download every new application, join every new social media platform, and purchase every new gadget because everyone around us is doing the same. We see these devices as facilitating things no other era of humanity was able to do. And we believe we are all the better for it. We call it "advancement".

What does this "advancement" look like? Children walking to the bus stop in the morning, each with their head down as they stare into the glare of their smartphone, checking their social media accounts, while at least a quarter of them suffer from depression or anxiety. A bustling street at lunch break, filled with busy professionals, professors, and CEOs texting and checking emails every few minutes, many of them plagued with stress, anxiety, or insomnia. A couple sitting on their couch, browsing through an online store, purchasing whatever they desire with the swipe of a finger, while their relationship has been suffering despite all their material possessions. An elderly person sleeping with their phone clutched in their hand with the TV flickering in and out, as it is their only way to stay "connected". A student sitting in class, chatting with someone hundreds of miles away while they ignore their teacher, only being able to focus on studying with the aid of medications. This is the picture of "advancement". Undoubtedly, these devices have allowed us to do what we were previously unable to do, but have we stopped seriously and asked what effects they have on us?

We live in an age of luxury, ease, and abundance, but at the same time we are plagued with depression, anxiety, addictions, and spiritual disconnect. We take advantage of the perceived benefits of the digital devices in our lives, but have we stopped to examine their real harms? Could they, perhaps, be contributing significantly to our physical and mental illnesses and spiritual void? Have they done more harm than good?

As the most beautifully spiritual and rational way of life, Islam calls us to carefully understand and weigh all the benefits and the harms of the choices we face before making any decisions. But have we critically analysed our digital choices, or have we followed others down this path without question? Our religion not only teaches us what to do, but also how to think. If we are to make more sound choices, we must not forget key Islamic foundational principles such as:

- weighing benefits and harms
- blocking the means to harm
- prioritising preventing harm over drawing benefit
- considering the effect of our decisions on those around us
- differentiating between necessities, needs, and conveniences, and
- looking to what has the most benefit for the Hereafter.

It is time to stop and see where our digital choices have led us. It is time for us to make more conscious choices. It is time for us to lead to a better path.

We know what you're thinking, we've heard it too. We used to think it as well, "This is just how the world is today, there is no other choice." And that is exactly the myth the developers of these devices would like us to believe, as we get pulled deeper and deeper into a virtual world, a virtual reality, all the while losing our sense of true reality.

> *It is time to stop and see where our digital choices have led us.*

The truth is that there is another alternative, there is another way. We need not be enslaved by these devices. We can, in fact, be successful and engage in the modern world while better maintaining our humanity. This book offers seekers of the Divine in the modern age a roadmap for doing so. But it begins with breaking misconceptions, understanding the real nature of these digital devices and platforms, and learning the skills necessary to navigate the digital age.

In the first half of the book, over four chapters, we examine the perceived benefits of devices and platforms alongside the actual harms that they cause, including a chapter on the dangerous culmination of these technologies with the development of Artificial Intelligence. In the second half of the book, over four chapters, we present a practical discussion with specific recommendations and suggestions for us all on how to better engage with digital communication means and thrive in the digital age.

We pray that Allah accepts this humble work and makes it purely for His sake. And all success is only from Allah.

PERCEIVED BENEFITS, REAL HARMS

1

The Common Narrative...
Breaking Misconceptions

Digital communication tools have revolutionised and transformed many aspects of life, from how we work, how we receive an education, how we socialise, and even how we find a spouse. Life itself has almost become unthinkable without some degree of interaction with these technologies. At face value, it seems like they have been mostly a force for good in the world. However, Islam provides us with a sophisticated framework to holistically assess harm and benefit and to judge for ourselves whether that is true or not.

This is even more important when many of the benefits are apparent, and many of the harms are more subtle thus making it more difficult to make informed decisions about our use of devices and to avoid unintended consequences. The point here is not to argue that digital communication tools have no real benefits whatsoever, but rather to challenge some of the most commonly cited benefits and argue that overall they are not as valuable as they are presented to be. Let us examine some arguments in favour of today's digital devices and applications, with a deeper discussion of the underlying realities that are often overlooked:

- "They help me be more productive."
- "They increase my knowledge."
- "They save me time."
- "They keep me connected."
- "They help me save my memories."
- "They give me more freedom."
- "They are a necessity in today's world."
- "They are neutral tools that can be used for good or bad."

"They help me be more productive."

Smartphones, with their easy access to news channels, emails and instant messaging apps, result in a jumble of work, family, friends, news and more, all happening simultaneously. While we respond to a work email, we receive a trivial notification about a friend, at the same time that our family member is messaging us about a serious matter, and all while news and weather reports are popping up on the screen. It makes us feel that we can be much more productive when we multitask.

This is a myth. Part of why we have come to embrace bundling digital tools and devices is due to our mistaken idea of multitasking. We believe we can now be much more time efficient and accomplish more tasks in a shorter period of time. Perhaps we can listen to Qur'an, while checking emails on the phone, while texting regarding an important community event, while answering a call from our colleague, taking a picture of the project we are working on and sending it all in the same window of time. Isn't this better and more efficient? The answer is no, it is not.

Psychologists have now realised there is no such thing as multitasking. The brain actually just jumps from one task to another back and forth, over and over again.[1] In essence what we perceive as multitasking is actually causing our brain to decrease its ability to focus on any one matter for an extended period of time, resulting in a pattern of brain activity similar to someone with Attention Deficit Disorder. Even though we lose on quality, at least it saves time, right? Actually, studies have found it does not, and in fact, tasks take longer, as the brain takes more time to switch between tasks over and over again[2] and that those who multitask make **more** errors and retain **less** information.

> *" Psychologists have now realised there is no such thing as multitasking. "*

Productivity is not just a matter of quantity, but also quality. A factory may produce 100 products in a short space of time, but if they are of no value, they cannot be sold. Another factory may produce half that amount in the same time, but they are all of tremendous value and sell out. Which factory manager is more productive? As we manage the tasks in our life and work, how is our productivity? Are we developing things of value? Modern digital devices and platforms give us the ability to multitask, but multitasking doesn't save time, nor does it improve the quality of what we produce. These devices simply distract and decrease productivity.

---

1   "Why Multitasking Is a Myth That's Breaking Your Brain and Wasting …," September 28, 2017, https://www.entrepreneur.com/article/299029
2   "Multitasking: Switching costs," March 20, 2006, https://www.apa.org/research/action/multitask

In the past, we had separate devices for each task, such as a phone for making calls, a computer for study and office work, a camera to capture special events. These devices had a specific limited purpose that we used at a specific time and place.

Today, our smartphone is our telephone, computer, email, internet, camera, source of learning, Qur'an, *dhikr* counter, banking centre, navigation system, and entertainment. In short, we are lost without it.

What are the implications of this on the human mind and soul? Were we meant to be able to do everything all at once at any time and in any place? Since physical elements and tasks in our life no longer have their own sacred place, time, and boundaries, and have all come together into one melting pot of ease and convenience, so too have our thoughts. It is no longer easy to sit and focus on one matter at a time, or focus on one task without thinking of the ten other tasks we are able to perform at our fingertips at that very moment.

If we designate special times and places for tasks, we will find our thoughts will also have their time and place.

So when we are talking to a family member on a simple phone, our thoughts will be focused on them. When we are working on a project for school, our mind will be focused on the project. When we are in *dhikr* of Allah, our heart will be focused on The One. Many of us seek to improve the quality of our concentration and presence within the prayer. As a first step, we could reflect on how we are outside of the *salah* because that is how we will be inside of *salah*. If our thoughts are scattered outside of *salah*, that is how they will be inside of *salah*.

The bottom line is that these tools do not actually make us more productive, they only make us *feel* more productive.

"They increase my knowledge."

With the proliferation of Islamic content available to us through every channel, it is easy to justify the amount of time we spend on our devices as gaining knowledge because we are listening to the Qur'an, we are learning from a scholar about aspects of our faith, our feed sends us daily reminders about religion.

While that may be the case, there is a difference between knowing more facts and information versus acquiring true deep knowledge. People today are inundated with facts, but has it increased us in beneficial knowledge that transforms our hearts? Has it increased our knowledge of Allah and our relationship with Him in a practical way? Allah continually asks us in the Qur'an to think, to ponder, to reflect, to look at the world around us and see His signs. These are meant to increase us in true spiritual insight, that leads to actions beloved to Him. This requires patience, focus, reflection, and practice. Many of our digital devices and applications habituate the opposite. When we use devices over prolonged periods of time, it impacts our ability to focus, to be still with our own feelings, to reflect and to ponder, until we lose those skills. Unable to think deeply, the quality of all of our actions is naturally compromised, including social and spiritual ones. In this agitated state, is it possible to be mindful, to have presence of heart in any of our actions? Can we expect our children that grow up with these devices to sit with focus in an hour-long class of knowledge?

This may seem like a small matter, but ultimately it leads to a lack of focus and orientation of the heart to Allah. The comfort of being alone with Allah – that deep connection with Him alone – is slowly chipped away and replaced with an addictive need to be with virtual others. True beneficial knowledge leads us to increase our certainty and conviction, increase our love and awe of the Divine, our love for the Prophet ﷺ, for the righteous, and for the Hereafter. Despite all the information available at our fingertips however, we find many of our youth and adults today suffer from the opposite: doubts, lack of conviction, and weakened faith. Has the abundance of information increased our love, fear, awe, hope, and gratitude of Allah? Has our following and love for the Prophet ﷺ increased?

The reality is that these digital devices and applications are, in many cases, actual distractions from Divine Oneness.

"They save me time."

A true believer is supposed to be the owner of his or her time and thus give every moment its right. So can we reasonably assume that if we use devices to get more done, then we can spend more time in worship, more time with family, and have more time for other beneficial works?

No. These ubiquitous screens waste our lives. While we are busy in our superficial, messaging, scrolling and chatting, we have forgotten how to be present in the real moment with its personal conversations, sights, sounds, connection with spiritual state and awareness of feeling. We are missing out on the most precious moments of our lives.

And how much time do devices actually save us? For example, it is indeed faster to send a text or chat message compared to making a phone call. However, the reality is the message usually receives a reply, which in turn needs another reply, until we find that we have spent 15 or 20 minutes in back and forth messaging, when the same information could have been conveyed more personally and effectively in a 2 or 3 minute voice conversation. This issue is exponentially exacerbated in chat groups.

Also, unlike a phone call or physical visit, which has a discrete beginning and end, messaging is a continuous flow, sometimes with no defined end. Our mind moves from one message to the next. In between, there is a distracting anticipation for the next message as the brain awaits the next high. This high we experience each time a new message pings through increases until we feel disappointed when we check our device and there is no new message. At that point, we may find something unnecessary to say or comment on, because we have become addicted to the communication medium itself.

Modern day digital devices and social media platforms have been designed to be addictive, as we shall explore in detail later. Addictions pull us away from priorities in life, rob us of time and bring us lower than the noble status that God has given us: "We have indeed honoured the children of Adam" (Qur'an 17:70).

The average adult will spend 44 (yes, that says 44!) years of their life staring at screens.[3] We have become conditioned to not tolerate any down time to reflect or ponder and instead, we instantly pick up our phone for a fix.[4] The result is half a lifetime or more of missed moments, as real life passes us by.

As servants on a mission to our Lord, do we want to embrace outright attacks on our most valuable asset? YouTube runs, endless scrolling, hours of chatting and texting – do these tools save us time, or rob us of it?

"They keep me connected."

The developers of these devices and programs argue that their mission is to "connect" people. How true is that statement and what are the pitfalls of "connection"?

---

3   "Average U.S. Adult Will Spend Equivalent of 44 Years of Their Life Staring at Screens: Poll," June 3, 2020, https://people.com/human-interest/average-us-adult-screens-study/

4   "Tech and Screen Addiction: Dr. David Greenfield," October 11, 2019, https://www.youtube.com/watch?v=IZLFCLbQ1no

It is obvious during any gathering of even practising Muslims, whether amongst friends or family or strangers, to see adults and children alike consistently engaged with their phones on some level as opposed to meaningfully interacting with people within the gathering for any length of time.

> **What about our connection to the natural world?**

The quantity of communication we are engaging in is undoubtedly increasing, but what about the quality? We have increased our virtual connections, but what is the strength of our connections with those around us? Are we actually fulfilling our responsibilities towards family members or do we think that we have done our part by sending a quick message? How often are we in the same room "with" our spouse and children where each of us is in our own virtual world engaging in meaningless or at least unnecessary interactions with others outside the home?

Allah describes believers as those who leave excessive and frivolous conversation (Qur'an 23:3), while the Prophet ﷺ taught us: "All the speech of the son of Adam is against him, not for him, except calling to good, forbidding wrong, or remembrance of Allah" (Ahmed).

The more unnecessary matters we engage in, the more this leads to the hardening of our heart, the committing of more sins, and ultimately having a longer list to account for on the Day of Resurrection. He ﷺ also taught: "Whoever believes in Allah and the Day of Judgement, then let him speak good, or otherwise be silent" (Bukhari). We know that the Prophet ﷺ himself "observed silence for long periods of time" (Ahmed). Based on these traditions of the Prophet ﷺ, Imam al-Shafi'i said the *Sunna* (Prophetic way) and default state of a believer is silence and there is great wisdom in this.

Chat groups and social media platforms encourage quite the opposite, where in many cases, there is excessive back and forth communication between many people sometimes simply to fulfil an egotistical drive to be seen and heard. How many times have disagreements or misunderstandings escalated on these chats and resulted in discord between people? Even when you do not personally comment, you end up reading scrolls of comments on multiple groups intermittently throughout the day. Is this the best use of time?

Another drawback to "connections" is the ease with which these devices and apps open avenues for unnecessary intermingling between the genders that is not in the spirit of Islamic shyness and modesty (*hayā'*). It is much easier to cross boundaries through the simple movement of a finger on a chat than it is by phone or in person. Imagine the equivalent of this before the digital age: private notes being passed back and forth between a man and a woman. This sort of "e-mixing" is not healthy for the hearts of those involved and neither is it healthy for the building of a faithful community, especially when there is no true need for this type of interaction. Even if you do not fear the probable harm from this practice for yourself, what is the example we are leaving for teenage boys and girls around us? Imagine having such unrestricted access to the opposite gender at that age, in the midst of trying to control our physical desires: it is almost spiritual suicide.

What about our connection to the natural world? Do we have one? Do we even realise the importance of having one? Adults and children alike walk from building to vehicle back to building looking down at a screen, missing the wondrous world around them. The sun, the moon, the stars, the trees, the flowers, the butterflies – all magnificent creations that point to the beauty and majesty of the Creator and affirm our faith. What is the effect on our hearts and minds and bodies as we disconnect from the natural world and immerse in a virtual one? And most importantly, how is our connection with Allah and His Messenger ﷺ?

Consider the choice some people make to chat, call, or digitally record moments at the Holy Precinct of the Ka'bah or in front of the noble resting place of the Prophet Muhammad ﷺ instead of fully living those most precious moments. People sometimes even turn their backs to these holy sites in order to take a selfie to post later on. If this scene does not bother us at some level, then we may need to recalibrate our spiritual sensitivity.

Overall, these digital tools simply dilute our meaningful connections with those around us, with nature and ultimately with Allah and His Messenger ﷺ, all the while giving us the illusion that we are more connected than ever.

"They help me save my memories."

With increasingly powerful cameras and videos in our pockets, it has never been easier to document our lives, to have a record of every moment of our children growing up, videos of our family gatherings, holidays and outings.

In fact, many of our important life moments are viewed from behind a screen. When we see something we like, we take a picture of it. Instead of experiencing life, we video it. We record our Eid celebrations, our children's first moments, their graduation days, weddings, the Islamic gatherings we attend. Whenever we are experiencing anything that is slightly meaningful to us, we reach for our phones.

How many photos did people take 20 years ago when the camera was its own device that you had to bring with you for a specific event? Now, with a camera at our disposal at all times, how many photos do we take? How many of those are unnecessary and excessive? How much time is being spent in trying to capture memories on a device while missing out on enjoying the moment itself, which will come to pass and never return? How much privacy has been invaded when people take pictures of everything and everyone without their permission?

As for the argument that pictures will help us to save our memories, studies have actually shown that people who capture experiences with a camera will have less recollection of the memory as compared to those who don't.[5] Are we capturing memories or losing them?

"They give me more freedom."

The word "freedom" is vaguely seen as an ideal state we should all aspire to, but what does it actually mean? Freedom to do what and from what? Is the ability to do anything – beautiful or ugly – at any time, the freedom we seek? Is the freedom of unlimited minutes, unlimited data, and unlimited access to information good for a *nafs* (self) that knows no limits?

On the contrary, the believer finds ways to put limits on their *nafs*; to be free *from* it as opposed to granting *it* freedom. This is one of the core purposes of our acts of worship. This is what the internal struggle against the base self is all about, which is a key aspect in the path to Allah. Our goal must not be to simply make everything convenient and accessible for the *nafs*, our goal is to gain mastery over the *nafs*.

It is in our nature to cross the limits if boundaries are not placed, as Allah explains: "And if Allah had extended [excessive] provision for His servants, they would have transgressed throughout the earth. But He sends [it] down in an amount He wills. Indeed He is, of His servants, All-Aware, All-Seeing" (Qur'an 42:27).

If a person knows they have a problem with over-eating and its effects on them, they will choose to stay away from an open-buffet restaurant. Yes, perhaps a very disciplined person can go and stop eating when their

---

5   Nicholas Carr, *The Shallows*, 2010

stomach is half-full, but are most people that disciplined? If a person is an excessive shopper and shops for the sake of shopping, it is better that they avoid a seemingly unlimited shopping mall. The same applies to technology usage. We need limits placed upon us for our own spiritual, mental, social and even physical well-being.

This is an understanding that more and more people are gaining in a bid for true freedom. Justin Rosenstein, former Facebook developer, "purchased a new iPhone and instructed his assistant to set up a parental-control feature to prevent him from downloading any apps. He was particularly aware of the allure of Facebook 'likes', which he describes as 'bright dings of pseudo-pleasure' that can be as hollow as they are seductive." He also "tweaked his laptop's operating system to block Reddit, banned himself from Snapchat, which he compares to heroin, and imposed limits on his use of Facebook…. It is revealing that many of these younger technologists are weaning themselves off their own products, sending their children to elite Silicon Valley schools where iPhones, iPads and even laptops are banned."[6]

Digital devices and platforms are designed to be addictive, generate addictions in users, and further prey on weakness and desires. Addictions of any type bend the natural human state (*fitra*) away from its Creator. Whatever the addiction may be – heroin, alcohol, food, emails, chatting, or social media – the end result is the same: a soul imprisoned and shackled from being able to freely travel to its Lord.

As believers, rather than giving the *nafs* instant access to an array of harms, we seek to put barriers between us and the things we may fall weak to. We look to understand what truly liberates and what enslaves us.

---

6 "'Our Minds Can Be Hijacked': The Tech Insiders Who Fear a Smartphone," October 6, 2017, https://www.theguardian.com/technology/2017/oct/05/smartphone-addiction-silicon-valley-dystopia

"They are a necessity in today's world."

To understand this argument, we must first properly define the term "necessity". Drawing from the terminology used by Islamic scholars in deducing legal verdicts, we learn that in life there are necessities, needs, and conveniences.

Necessities are realities without which we cannot sustain human life, such as access to clean water, a roof and walls for shelter, and freedom to practise the essentials of religion like *salāh* (prayer). Without necessities, life cannot exist.

Needs, on the other hand, are realities without which life would be unnecessarily difficult. Examples may include warm water in cold environments or having a door to our home.

Conveniences are realities that decorate our life. They make life easier or more beautiful. These include running water *within* our home, windows to allow sunlight, and exposure to beautiful characteristics such as generosity and humility. Some realities may be a necessity for someone but a need or a convenience for another, and so on.

For most people, many of the devices and apps used cannot be categorised as necessities. Claiming that they are necessities would be claiming that without them life would be unsustainable, miserable or unbearable, which is clearly not true. Most apps and devices are conveniences or at most, in some cases, needs.

Many people who have chosen to voluntarily go without their devices or certain apps, have actually discovered that they are perfectly fine without them. In fact, quality of life increases, even for those individuals who are successful, ambitious and busy in the worldly sense. Both our children and we can survive and thrive intellectually, physically, and, most importantly, spiritually and morally without a smartphone, without 24/7 access to the internet, without video games, and without social media accounts.

Shaytān (Satan) and his impact on the human base *nafs* makes reality appear altered. He will make it seem that we cannot, as a matter of necessity, perform *Salāh* in our workplace or ask for leave to attend Friday prayers (*Jumu'ah*). He will make it seem that we cannot live in today's world without accepting some of the very vile and ugly norms that have appeared in the last few decades. The challenge of the believer is to see past these superficial façades and recognise everything for what it truly is. There are necessities in life, but the reality is that the vast majority of our interaction with the digital world does not fall within that category.

Sometimes it takes forcing one's nafs to temporarily let go of something in life to see how unnecessary it really is.

When internal conflict arises, necessities always take precedence over needs, which take precedence over conveniences. If necessary aspects of our connection with Allah, controlling our *nafs,* nourishing our intellect, maintaining our honour and reputation and serving our family are suffering as a result of our interaction with the digital world, then we cannot continue to engage in what is convenient at the expense of what is necessary.

Are our digital practices necessities, or is this simply rhetoric that has been repeated over and over to make us believe what is not?

"They are neutral tools that can be used for good or bad."

A popular argument is that these digital means are simply tools that may be used for good and bad, and initially that argument seems to hold some merit. However, if we look with a more critical spiritual and rational eye, we will discover that this argument is not accurate for a number of reasons.

They are addictive by design: The companies that develop these devices employ specialised psychological tools built into their platforms to habituate users for the benefit of corporations who have no concern for our well-being or the well-being of our family.[7,8] Many of the top programmers, developers, and tech companies around the world gather each year to attend a conference on how to manipulate people into becoming addicted to their products. The host of the "Habit Summit", as it is called, has even written his own book on the subject, *Hooked: How to Build Habit Forming Products*.

Facebook's former president, Sean Parker, commenting on the platform, says, "It literally changes your relationship with society, with each other. It probably interferes with productivity in weird ways. God only knows what it's doing to our children's brains." He also explains that as they were first developing Facebook their objective was, "How do we consume as much of your time and conscious attention as possible?"[9]

By simply reflecting on our own experiences, we can see to what extent this is true in our own lives. How many times have we finished sending that message or watching that video while our *salāh* gets delayed? How many times have we been on the phone while ignoring

---

7 Adam Alter, *Irresistible*, 2017
8 Shoshana Zuboff, *The Age of Surveillance Capitalism*, 2019
9 "Ex-Facebook President Sean Parker: Site Made to Exploit Human ...," November 9, 2017, https://www.theguardian.com/technology/2017/nov/09/facebook-sean-parker-vulnerability-brain-psychology

> **we just need to ask ourselves how uneasy we would feel if we were told to give up our smartphone for a week**

our child's need for attention and their right to simply have us be present for them? How many times have we suddenly and rudely ignored the person speaking with us to read the new message we just received? How many times have we sat in a gathering and decided to fiddle with our phone? How many times did we choose to walk while engaging with our phone instead of reflecting, pondering, and experiencing our real surroundings? How many times did we choose to drive and text knowing the risk of a fatal accident?

The list goes on, but this should be enough for an honest seeker of truth to understand that most of us are already addicted. Research has shown that the use of these programs and devices restructures the brain, as we will come to see in Chapter Two.

People touch their smartphone screen on average 2,617 times a day, and heavy users over 5,000 times a day.[10] What would be the impact if even a fraction of those touches were replaced with touches of the pages of the Qur'an? Or one movement of prayer beads? Or a gaze at our child or parent to give them the attention they need? What would the cumulative effect be on a society? And what is the cumulative effect on a society busied with 2,600 touches of their smartphones daily?

---

10 "Putting a Finger on Our Phone Obsession," June 16, 2016, https://blog.dscout.com/mobile-touches

If any one of us still doubts whether or not we are overly attached to our devices, we just need to ask ourselves how uneasy we would feel if we were told to give up our smartphone for a week and just use a simple phone and computer instead?

For the sake of comparison, let us look at the example of another tool: a hammer. Arguably, a hammer is a neutral tool, and it can be used to build a house or hurt someone, and that it is up to the user how they use the tool. While we can correctly say that a hammer is a neutral tool, that is not true of a smartphone. Have you ever come across someone addicted to a hammer? The answer, of course, is no. Why not? Because it wasn't designed with the intent to get people addicted to its use. A neutral tool such as a hammer does not manipulate you, demand of you, nor seduce you. A hammer doesn't break up families or ruin mental health.

What we must finally come to see is that smartphones, messaging apps, social media, video games, and internet surfing platforms were designed with the purpose to get people addicted and glued to them as much as possible, regardless of the content or use.

Even if we are doing something important on a device, what we may not realise is that these tools are re-wiring our brain all the time we are using them, activating addictive neuronal pathways, developing neurochemical imbalances, and ultimately resulting in a brain and soul that is out of balance. Why, we might ask, would anyone design such products?

The answer is that we are being used through engineered addictions to generate wealth for others and for our personal data to be bought, sold, and traded for other purposes, which will be explored in Chapter Three.

Even if we choose not to use these digital means to access explicitly harmful or unlawful material or activities, even if we think that we can control the amount of time we spend on our devices, there are still inherent harms that we are involuntarily being exposed to regardless of what we are using our phones for, some of which are:

They limit our potential: What if you used that hammer at all times for all the tasks in your life? Yes, you can build objects, but what if you used it to communicate emotions, and slammed it down on a table to display anger? Or what if you gently tapped someone on the head with it to show your affection? Or if you used it to write with?

On the other hand, what can the human voice be used to communicate? What range of emotions, sounds, expressions, and meanings can it convey? Or how about the handwritten word composed with a pen? Now compare that to communicating using 26 keys on a keyboard or screen. This imposes immediate limitations and attributes on what is communicated. Now limit that further to a chat box, or messaging app and we lose the rich and beautiful range of communication that we are capable of, that no amount of emojis can replace. The inherent nature of digital means dictate the nature of the information we communicate and thus in many ways limit our potential.

They cause us to become heedless: Part of a Muslim's challenge is to see through the fleeting enjoyment of delusions, which are the characteristics of this world we live in and into what is everlasting and more real. "But the life of this world is nothing but an enjoyment of delusion" (Qur'an 3:185). "Nay, you prefer the life of this world, whereas the Hereafter is better and more lasting" (Qur'an 87:16-17).

Even in the most exquisite surroundings of this world, a believer should not be trapped spiritually and intellectually in the realities he or she is experiencing, but to use them to see meaning behind that creation, to ponder on the Hereafter and, most importantly, to connect with the Creator. However, the virtual world, in many cases, veils us from these reflections and we enter into an even deeper layer of deception. We are distanced from Allah by yet another degree and we become even more heedless.

They make us vulnerable to corruption: We may be innocently posting our pictures and sharing harmless information online, but if this gets into the wrong hands then it has the potential to facilitate cyber crime such as cyber bullying, identity theft, fraud and extortion, to name a few.

The advent of DeepFake technology[11] enables individuals with bad intentions to potentially use your genuinely posted images, videos and audios to produce fake virtual representations of you. How much harm is already being done by using the images and voices of innocent people to show them doing or saying the most vile of things or to deceive and commit crimes?

So widespread is this phenomenon that it is no longer possible to believe anything that you see or hear in the virtual world. The statement attributed to the mentor you follow may not be true. The video you see may be fake. The account you follow may be hacked. Additionally, there is always the danger that someone can hack into your account and attribute things to you that you did not say or do.

This is a serious state of *fitna* (trial) where it is becomes much more difficult to distinguish between truth and falsehood and has the potential to be a source of much evil, and ultimately the deterioration of populations intellectually, morally and most importantly, spiritually.

They expose our shortcomings: The attraction of social media platforms is the ease with which we can convey our thoughts to a wide audience. We all have passing thoughts and emotions and these are best dealt with through an internal process of reflection, analysis and modification to filter out those that originate from satanic whispers and the *nafs*.

Instead, we can give those thoughts an unfiltered and immediate presence on a global centre stage by sharing them in the moment, at

---

[11] "When seeing is no longer believing: Inside the Pentagons race against deep fakes," https://www.cnn.com/interactive/2019/01/business/pentagons-race-against-deepfakes/

which point we lose control over their consequence. By receiving 'likes', our flimsiest comments and thoughts are strengthened and endorsed without the regulation process that is needed for us to elevate ourselves as human beings.

Face to face, people will talk about themselves about 30% of the time. However, on social media, people talk about themselves almost 80% of the time.[12] So these platforms are often simply a means to inflate the ego and, therefore, hinder spiritual growth.

When we rush to post that picture or tweet that comment, we are leaving a sort of permanent record of our current opinions, feelings, actions, and appearance, however temporary or impulsive they may be. Do we really want to permanently save all of this on other people's devices, accessible to an untold number of third parties?

In the past someone may have authored a well thought out book or written a letter, and that would be the extent of the record they left behind. However, today so much of our mundane thoughts and casual photos are being stored indefinitely. As we go through life, we go through changes in the way we speak, how we act, how we look, what we believe. How many of us grow intellectually and spiritually and realise that the previous state is not one that we still want to be identified with? The emotion that we expressed yesterday may have been in a moment of ignorance or anger, not to be something that is forever attached to us.

It is true that Allah records our every action, thought, and feeling but He covers our faults and erases them. He is *Al-Sittir* (The One Who Conceals) and *Al-'Afuw* (The One Who Erases). Can we guarantee these characteristics at any level for others who have a massive record of our written words, our voice, and our images?

---

12 "40+ frightening social media and mental health statistics," November 12,2020, https://etactics.com/blog/social-media-and-mental-health-statistics

They affect our mental health: Studies have shown that leading a life predominately online engaged in social media is a cause of increased anxiety, depression, and insomnia. Users are constantly living a life of comparing themselves to others, resulting in chronic displeasure and discontentment.[13,14,15]

Even healthy or somewhat neutral usage can become unhealthy and negative through excessive use as it starts to take priority over what is truly important. We live in an age of information overload. Unfortunately today, many of us lack the standards and essential skills to properly process information. Seekers of information, instead of being enlightened, find themselves overloaded with information of varying degrees of relevance and accuracy only to be left with a confused mind and conflicted heart.

> *the real world does not work with swipes and clicks, but with patience, hard work and supplication*

They affect our spiritual health: Digital means have other subtle, negative effects on our spiritual states, such as decreasing patience (*sabr*), Divine reliance (*tawakkul*) and aspiration (*himmah*). For example, we may have a harder time waiting with patience to speak to someone in person because we have grown used to instantly sending and receiving

---

13 "Increased social media use linked to developing depression, research finds," December 10, 2020, https://news.uark.edu/articles/55480/increased-social-media-use-linked-to-developing-depression-research-finds

14 "Social media use linked to anxiety, depression among teens, new study finds," January 9, 2020, https://www.wbur.org/hereandnow/2020/01/09/social-media-anxiety-depression-teens

15 "2019 Children's Mental Health Report," Child Mind Institute, https://childmind.org/awareness-campaigns/childrens-mental-health-report/2019-childrens-mental-health-report/

a text message. Why pray for our family member's safe arrival and practise more reliance when they are late, if we can text them instead? Imagine that the *Ansār* (Madinan Helpers) would not have gone out in the beautiful act of worship of waiting with expectation for the Prophet's ﷺ arrival from Makkah if they could have just viewed his live location on their smartphones.

In addition, virtual reality offers us a trigger-happy culture where we can casually change realities at the click of a button. This perceived control leaves us less equipped to deal with the real world which does not work with swipes and clicks, but with patience, hard work and supplication, all of which we are finding harder to put into action.

The Principle of What is Most Likely

Of course not everyone who has a smartphone or other digital devices will struggle with all of these harms. These are not necessary consequences of these devices, but what is likely for most people.

Drawing from the Islamic legal maxim that verdicts are based on what is most probable and not on rarities, we learn a very valuable and straightforward principle to live by: when we make decisions, we should make them based upon the most likely scenarios and not rare ones. Yes, of course there are people with enormous self-discipline, fuelled by their spiritual and intellectual state, that are able to use digital devices and apps and avoid the worst of the consequences that come with these tools. However, this is the exception and not the rule. In the face of very strongly financed and engineered tactics to create addictive products, most people will fall prey to much of the harm the digital world has to offer and most people will not be able to pull the brakes before crossing over from the neutral to the negative.

How many video game users nowadays decide to play relatively only mild games? How many children, teens, and adults, on the other hand, play video games where they are controlling a person who casually kills or injures random people they encounter in the most gruesome of ways? How then do we expect that user to be sensitive to human suffering or display any degree of empathy?

How many of the many millions of social media posts out there are truly beneficial? How many inappropriate or useless posts do we have to avoid to get to those of true benefit? And how many times have we become side tracked and involved in mindless engagement?

The internet, whether accessed by a computer or smartphone has become a means to access literally every shade of evil offered to mankind. That is because this medium is predominately managed by individuals who have no sense of Divine limits and thus no concern for people's spiritual states or ultimate conditions in the Hereafter.

At no point in history has it been the case that the ugliest of thoughts, sounds, and images are literally in people's pockets all the time. How many of us can honestly say that we would never fall in the face of such free access?

It is part of the beauty of Islam that Allah has prevented us from even going near that which will cause us to fall. Not only does He command us not to commit adultery, for example, He commands us to not even approach it (Qur'an 17:32). For even approaching some sins is so harmful and damaging to individuals and society that all that leads to it is forbidden.

In our beautiful and balanced *Shari'ah* (Islamic law), a person is not permitted to stare at someone of the opposite gender, even if they are appropriately covered, without a legally sanctioned reason. This serves the higher purpose of protecting hearts and society. If this is the standard of our faith, then how can we justify exposing ourselves and our children to the constant bombardment of imagery that social media is? How many websites, social media platforms, and video games are free of sin and impurity?

One very alarming so-called advancement of our digital world is the advent of an online virtual reality world: the metaverse. Facebook, in hopes that virtual reality will be the next medium to replace the internet, has rebranded its company as Meta.

Jaron Lanier, the computer scientist credited as the father of virtual reality, offers some dark words on the subject: "If you run [the metaverse] on a business model that's similar to the one that Facebook runs on, it'll destroy humanity. I'm not saying that rhetorically. That is a literal and specific prediction that humanity could not survive that."[16]

As if it were not enough that all the evil present in the world is sitting in our pocket, with the advent of virtual reality, it will be something we will be able to completely immerse ourselves in. Through virtual goggles we will now be able to more intensely experience the online world and all the harm it has to offer. One way to understand the harms coming from this wave is to simply multiply the harms we have just discussed exponentially. If we, as parents, fear what our children may be exposed to in front of a computer screen, just imagine what they will now be exposed to within it.

An experiment conducted by the BBC shows the vile experiences a child in the metaverse will likely come in contact with.[17] Those parents who painstakingly try to protect their children from spiritually and morally harmful environments will now have those same environments engulfing

---

16 "What is the metaverse, and why does Mark Zuckerberg care so much about it," November 3, 2021, https://www.forbes.com/sites/abrambrown/2021/11/03/zuckerberg-facebook-metaverse-meta-virtual-reality-oculus/?sh=583c432e6b69

17 "Metaverse app allows kids into virtual strip clubs," February 23, 2022, https://www.bbc.com/news/technology-60415317

their lives and their children's lives in unprecedented ways. But then again, unfortunately as is the case for much of the harm in the digital world, Muslims will, by and large, be amongst the average statistics. Many people will point at some of the perceived or even real benefits that come along with these major harms and casually consume whatever is offered. Any intelligent observer can simply and clearly see that the digital harms will only get worse. If we do not pull the brakes now, and make some serious decisions, when will we?

It is important to note that this is not an argument against technology in a general sense. It is true that social media plays a positive role in many ways including uncovering global truths in a world where many news stations are no longer credible. However, the same platform, for example, that helped expose the barbaric actions of the IDF in Palestine also was a tool for genocide in Myanmar, as we shall look at in more detail in the next chapter. The startling reality is that the more we understand the reality of modern digital practices, the more we realise that these devices and programs are not neutral tools. They will always have a negative effect on us, at some level, regardless of what we are using them for.

We also must keep in mind that as many of us are parents, teachers, or serving as some sort of role model for others, we must be extra cautious to ensure that we model the utmost level of moral character when it comes to our digital choices. It is not sufficient to simply choose what we think is best for us alone, we must also look at the probable consequences that will affect those who emulate us either by choice or out of necessity due to their relationship with us.

What can we expect to naturally occur to the heart of our child when we choose to walk around most of the day at home with a smartphone? Are we ready for them to have this same addictive relationship with it? Whatever we preoccupy ourselves with is what they will attach themselves to as well.

> **If we don't pause, analyse, and make serious decisions today, when will we?**

Unlike us, our children have never experienced a world without these devices and thus have no reference to compare the present reality to. Unlike us, they cannot miss "the good old days" when people visited each other regularly, wrote letters to one another, picked up the phone and called when they needed something, and in general had a screen-free life. This lack of reference will cause them to be oblivious to what they are truly missing. As Justin Rosenstein put it: "One reason I think it is particularly important for us to talk about this now is that we may be the last generation that can remember life before."[18]

***

Looking back on the arguments and the harms presented, it is easy to give up and join the flow of whatever is happening around us. However, we must not forget that our current digital practices are predominately choices that we are making out of our own free will, albeit under the influence of highly effective marketing and behaviour modification technology. As spiritually and rationally intelligent people who are submitting to Allah, if we do not take a holistic view of these benefits and harms, who will? If we don't pause, analyse, and make serious decisions today, when will we? If we do not model a better quality of life, then how can we call others to the most pristine, spiritual, and rational system in existence, that is Islam?

---

18 "'Our Minds Can Be Hijacked': The Tech Insiders Who Fear a Smartphone," October 6, 2017, https://www.theguardian.com/technology/2017/oct/05/smartphone-addiction-silicon-valley-dystopia

2

Digital Addiction:
Impact on the Brain

What comes to mind when you think of an addict? A gaunt figure with a heroin addiction, in a back alley, looking for needles? A violent alcoholic, with their life spiralling out of control? These are not images we associate with our family members or expect our children to fall into. We see those images in movies, not in our day-to-day lives and so we often cannot relate to addiction or recognise it in our homes.

Addictions: One and the Same

Consider some of the symptoms you would expect in someone with an addiction:
- Compulsive use
- Dependence
- Isolation
- Distancing from family and friends
- Emotional instability
- Irritability
- Anger or agitation when separated from the addiction
- Losing track of time
- Falling behind on responsibilities
- Physical withdrawal symptoms.

While these symptoms of addiction can be found in those suffering from addictions of alcohol, drugs, gambling or pornography, they are also the exact symptoms found in those falling into an addiction with their digital devices and online platforms. While the former types of addiction are clear and obvious, the latter generally goes unnoticed. But make no mistake, whether it be alcohol, drugs, smartphones, messaging, social media, video games, they are all one and the same in many ways. The physiological changes in the brain are potentially the same. The effects on mental, physical, spiritual and emotional health are potentially the same. The destruction of family relationships, career aspirations and social circles is potentially the same.

> *" make no mistake, whether it be alcohol, drugs, smartphones, messaging, social media, video games, they are all one and the same in many ways. "*

The Dopamine Hijack

Within the brain are neuronal pathways, or super highways, where different parts of the brain communicate with each other. You may be looking to relax after a long day at work or school, and one part of your brain may reach out to another via these neuronal pathways to engage in a relaxing, pleasurable activity such as reading, exercising, going for a walk, sitting beside the lake, performing *salāh*, or remembering Allah (*dhikr*). Engaging in these healthy enjoyable activities releases a hormone in the brain called **dopamine,** which is responsible for helping us feel satisfaction and pleasure. Each time we engage in these activities dopamine is released, and the brain learns to seek those activities when looking for relaxation or satisfaction, and as a result those neuronal pathways become stronger.

What happens in an addiction? When someone engages in an unhealthy addictive behaviour (remember this could be alcohol or scrolling videos on social media), the signals of the brain travel along different neuronal pathways to seek out that behaviour. Those addictive behaviours release a large amount of dopamine – much larger than what is released when engaging in healthy behaviours. As a result, there is a strong physiological pull towards the unhealthy behaviour. The brain knows that when it wants to feel relaxed and satisfied, it can engage in an addictive behaviour and receive a much larger dopamine reward. Over time, the person is pulled more and more towards those addictive behaviours.

Neuronal pathways in the brain are just like streets and highways. The more they are used, the more ingrained they become. When a pathway is left abandoned, it starts to become covered with dirt and shrubs, and is no longer usable. After engaging in addictive behaviours for some time, the pathways that connect you with the rewards from healthy behaviours close off, and the pathways leading to unhealthy addictive behaviours strengthen and become more automatic.

Have you ever wondered why a teenager who spends hours a day playing video games finds no enjoyment whatsoever in playing outside or going fishing? Those natural healthy activities have become "boring" because physiologically their brain has changed. Devices and apps have been designed to be unpredictable, exciting, providing rapid response positive feedback to the user that gives them an immediate sense of accomplishment. Imagine hearing, "Congratulations! You have reached level 14" accompanied by a musical jingle and animation. You cannot get that level of instant gratification and validation from reading or going for a walk.

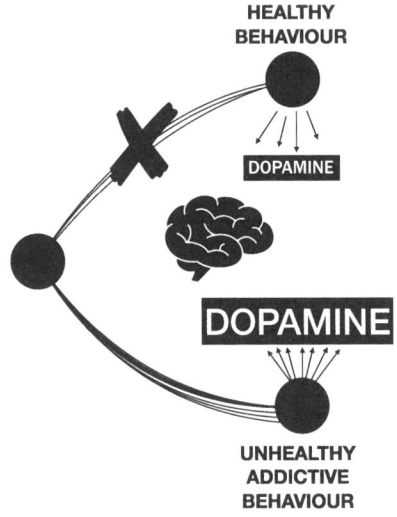

Faced with that, the brain can no longer access the dopamine produced from those natural healthy activities, as it has been pulled towards an addictive behaviour that produces all the dopamine needed. Even if there is some dopamine produced from reading or spending time in nature, it is short lived as it doesn't compare to the huge amounts of dopamine produced with video games or social media. Imagine a child who has grown up eating sugary sweets and candies regularly; the delicious taste of a crisp, juicy apple is completely lost on them.

This is the hijacking of the dopamine pathway. It is a physiological change that occurs in the brain of a person, regardless of their age, when they engage in addictive behaviours regularly: a young child addicted to YouTube videos, a teenager addicted to TikTok, a young professional addicted to their emails and chatting, a mother addicted to Candy Crush. These addictive behaviours pull people away from enjoying natural, healthy activities. Most importantly, they pull the soul away from finding bliss and pleasure in the remembrance and worship of Allah.

It has reached the point that Internet Addiction Disorder[19] is now a recognised condition and people have actually needed to seek clinical treatment for their digital addictions.[20,21]

The good news is that these changes can be reversed and undone even after many years. By removing addictive behaviours and replacing them with healthy ones, the pathways and dopamine release can be reset in the brain. Once the child is weaned off those sugary sweets, their taste buds will begin to appreciate again the balanced bite of a Honeycrisp apple.

Digital Imagery and the Brain

Aside from the addictive pathways induced mentioned above, there is another significant effect on the brain by simply viewing digital imagery.

When we look at a real object, our brain and senses are fully stimulated and engaged. The real object exists in a space and a context, with surrounding objects, sights, sounds, and smells. Light from the

---

19 "Internet Addiction Disorder - Signs, Symptoms, and Treatments," May 22, 2019, https://www.psycom.net/iadcriteria.html
20 "Inside the Rehab Saving Young Men from Their Internet Addiction ...," June 16, 2017, https://www.theguardian.com/technology/2017/jun/16/internet-addiction-gaming-restart-therapy-washington
21 "Should DSM-V Designate 'Internet Addiction' a Mental Disorder," February 2009, https://www.ncbi.nlm.nih.gov/pmc/articles/PMC2719452/

object reflects to our retinas in an array of colours and wavelengths. If we were to look at someone's eyes when they were looking at a real object, we would notice that their eyes are not fixed, but rather they are oscillating, and their pupils are constricting and dilating. These all indicate active attentive analysis. The brain is fully engaged.

If we were now to look at someone staring at a digital image on a screen, the picture is quite different. The range of eye movements significantly decreases and the pupils are fixed. This fixed glare is similar to what is observed in people in a hypnotic state.[22] The brain starts to mimic someone in sensory deprivation. Other surrounding stimuli fade out. The brain waves even begin to change from active beta waves to passive alpha and delta waves (alpha waves are present when you are awake but not processing much information, while delta waves are present in sleep). There is not the same active process present as when looking at a real object. Instead the brain enters a passive state.[23]

Why does this occur? If we look at what digital images are composed of, they are essentially dots, i.e. pixels. This collection of dots is not a real image, but rather something the subconscious mind has to piece together to form an image. So, the conscious mind is not able to latch on and analyse it in the same way it does with a real image. The collection of dots is pieced together in the subconscious mind, while the conscious critical mind is bypassed.[24] As a result, beta waves decrease, and alpha

---

22 Jerry Mander, *Four Arguments for the Elimination of Television*, 1978
23 Ibid
24 Ibid

and delta waves predominate. We can see this in the change of eye movements as well.

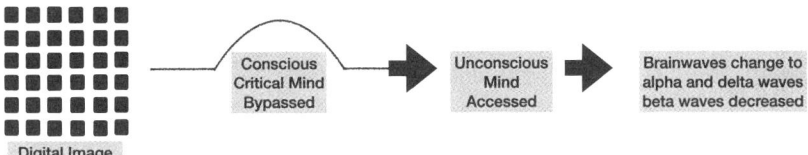

What is the effect of hours of staring at digital images and videos on a screen? The critical mind is inhibited and the prefrontal cortex is weakened. When we stare at digital images, a passive state is induced in us. On one hand, there is a certain type of stimulation of the brain, but any impulse to act is repressed. This "sensory tease" continues back and forth between stimulation and repression. Once a person disengages, all that repressed stimulation results in a state of hyperactivity. As Jerry Mander describes: "The physical energy which is created by images, but not used, is physically stored. Then when the set is off, it comes bursting outward in aimless, random, speedy activity."[25] This is most noticeable in children, who become quiet while watching a screen, then overactive, irritable, and frustrated afterwards. Next time you notice a child playing video games or watching a video on a screen, look out for the way their eyes are or how their behaviour is before, during and after their gaming session.

The Prefrontal Cortex

A specific part of the brain is especially sensitive to the effects of digital devices: the prefrontal cortex. This is involved in decision making, planning, executive function (the ability to plan and manage a series of tasks), self-control, reflexive behaviours and emotions.

25 Ibid

It will come as no surprise, given the symptoms of addiction we mentioned previously, to learn that addictions affect the prefrontal cortex.[26] Not only will they cause dysfunction of the prefrontal cortex, they will also induce atrophy, a decrease in size, of this critical part of the brain.[27] Years of addictions to video games, social media apps, emails, messages and so on take their physical toll on the brain. A person's decision making capacity, their ability to delay gratification, and regulate their emotional responses are all weakened. It is not only addictions that have this effect, but also hours of exposing the brain to digital images.

With the prefrontal cortex playing such a critical role in the brain, at what age does it fully develop? It develops from around 20 years of age, fully developing at about 25 years of age. This means that until it is fully developed, a person still makes decisions that are not completely based on reason, but rather may rely on other parts of the brain such as the amygdala, which is involved in emotions. Exposing children and young adults to addictive devices and platforms during the years of development of their prefrontal cortex is only harming them. Hours spent on video games, social media, smartphones, chatting apps are only inhibiting the development of their prefrontal cortex.

Bearing this in mind, is it wise to give a 12-year-old a PlayStation game console? Would it benefit the development of an 11-year-old to have a smartphone? *"But dad, everyone in school has one."* Unfortunately, everyone in school is also suffering the consequences of exposure to these digital devices. ADHD, anxiety, depression, insomnia, and suicide rates are all on the rise in children and adolescents. Mental health challenges are the leading cause of disability and poor health outcomes in young people. In the last decade, students who reported persistent feelings of sadness or hopelessness increased by 40%, to

---

26 Goldstein, Volkow, "Dysfunction of the prefrontal cortex in addiction: neuroimaging findings and clinical implications, " October 20, 2011, Nat Rev Neuroscience, 12 (11)

27 "Gray Matters: Too Much Screen Time Damages the Brain," February 27, 2014, https://www.psychologytoday.com/us/blog/mental-wealth/201402/gray-matters-too-much-screen-time-damages-the-brain

more than 1 in 3 students. Suicide rates among youth aged 10-24 in the U.S. increased by 57%.[28]

It is time to question the narrative that these devices and platforms are a necessary part of life. We saw in Chapter One that, for most people, they are not. They only hinder and hurt the beautiful phase of growing up. It is time to question the narrative that our children are mature enough to manage their online time, that they have grown up to be digitally smart. How is this possible when their decision making centre, the prefrontal cortex, is not yet fully developed and is actually being destroyed by the very thing we have handed to them?

The Internet's Effect on the Brain

Up until this point, we have been discussing the effect of digital devices and platforms on the brain. However, we cannot ignore the environment which ties all these devices together: the internet. As Nicholas Carr details in his groundbreaking book *The Shallows*, the internet itself is not a benign medium.

> *" The internet, by design, suppresses patience and concentration. "*

At the advent of the internet, supporters hailed it as a great vehicle that would provide unprecedented access to information and knowledge across the globe and become a means for us to become smarter and make better choices. Decades later, we find this is absolutely not the case.

---

28 "U.S. Surgeon General Issues Advisory on Youth Mental Health Crisis Further Exposed by COVID-19 Pandemic," December 7, 2021, https://www.hhs.gov/about/news/2021/12/07/us-surgeon-general-issues-advisory-on-youth-mental-health-crisis-further-exposed-by-covid-19-pandemic.html

> **We simply become "mindless consumers of data."**

Unlimited information and connectivity has resulted in an infinite scope of distraction, but our brain capacity is not unlimited. New information takes patience and concentration to process and evaluate. The internet, by design, suppresses patience and concentration. This stimulus overload results in attention splitting and superficial thinking. Prior to the internet, our minds were much more focused, undisturbed, and our thought processes were linear. The internet has changed that. We now think in short, disjointed, overlapping bursts.

Neuroscientists now understand that the brain is always in flux. Our daily habits, thoughts, and the tools we use actively shape our brain. The brain's ability to adapt, reorganise, form new nerve endings and synapses, and change is called **neuroplasticity.** This neuroplasticity can work for us and against us. Carr states, the "tools we use work on our mind as we work on them." Different types of technologies have varying levels of impact on the brain. The technologies that restructure language have the strongest influence on our intellectual lives. One such technology is the internet. The internet has completely changed the way we read, think, and process information. With the average person spending almost 7 hours online daily, its effects on the brain have been quite significant.[29]

When we go online, given the massive amount of information available, we enter an environment that necessitates and promotes cursory reading, hurried and distracted thinking, and as a result superficial learning. This has affected how we write as well. Carr explains

---

29 "10 Internet statistics every marketer should know in 2021," May 9 2021, https://www.oberlo.com/blog/internet-statistics

how "our indulgence in the pleasure of information and immediacy has led to the narrowing of experience and a loss of eloquence." The internet offers stimuli that result in strong rapid alterations in brain circuitry by bombarding us with repetitive, intensive, interactive, and addictive material and, as such, may be the most powerful mind altering technology. It "seizes our attention, only to scatter it."[30]

Book reading is a healthy process for the brain. It stimulates calm, linear thought, which is necessary for depth, reflection, and analysis. Screen reading changes the degree of attention and depth. Hyperlinks in the text cause the brain to continually shift focus, making split second decisions as to whether to click or not. Searchable fields fragment our thought processes. Websites that combine many types of multimedia, such as embedded audio/video, further fragment and distract.[31,32,33] As Cory Doctorow puts it: "Whenever we turn on our computers we are plunged into an ecosystem of interruption technologies."[34]

The internet's effect on how we process information has changed how information is delivered to us outside of the internet as well. Websites present material in a way that shortens our attention spans, and so we have become accustomed to processing information in this manner. As a result, companies produce products that are geared towards people with shorter attention spans. They are marketed to us in this manner as well. The use of these products and platforms further shorten our attention spans. This loop continues, as the world of fragmented attention on the internet has become the way we live and communicate and think outside of the internet.

---

30 Nicholas Carr, *The Shallows*, 2010
31 Miall, Dobson, "Reading Hypertext and the Experience of Literature," August 13, 2001, Journal of Digital Information 2,1
32 Niederhauser, Reynolds, Slamen, Skolmoski, "The Influence of Cognitive Load on Learning from Hypertext," Journal of Educational Computing Research 23, 3, 2000
33 DeStefano, LeFevre, "Cognitive Load in Hypertext Reading: A Review," September 30, 2005, Computers in Human Behavior, 23, 2
34 Nicholas Carr, *The Shallows*, 2010

This, in turn, has decreased our capacity to remember. Short term memory, our working memory, is a conscious memory. It is where we process information to move it to long term memory. Long term memory, in our subconscious, is accessed through bringing the memory back to our working memory. Information that flows from our working memory is referred to as our **cognitive load.** If our cognitive load is greater than our ability to store and process information, we cannot retain information or draw conclusions or connections with previous memories. The internet puts too much pressure on our working memory, not allowing consolidation of long term memory and thus causing us to become forgetful. It is designed to bombard us with information, to consume as much as possible in the shortest amount of time, far exceeding our cognitive load. We simply become "mindless consumers of data."[35] To handle this information overload, we have changed how we read: scanning, skimming, and multitasking.

The key to memory consolidation is attentiveness: concentration with repetition and intellectual or emotional engagement. Conscious attention begins in the frontal lobes of the cerebral cortex. In the midbrain, dopamine is produced, and then the hippocampus aids in memory consolidation. The internet blocks and diverts this whole process. It pushes us to process as much as possible in the shortest amount of time, constantly diverting our attention to something new. Our brains, to keep up, must become adept at forgetting. And so this is how we become even when we are away from our computers.

A related aspect is the effect on our range of human emotions. A calm, attentive mind is needed for empathy and compassion. Higher emotions evolve from neural processes that are inherently slow. The more distracted we become, the less capacity we have for empathy and subtle human emotions, thus affecting our social skills and relationships negatively.

---

35 Ibid

Interestingly, studies have shown that spending time in nature or being in rural settings close to nature results in people exhibiting increased attentiveness, stronger memories, and increased cognition.[36]

As the world plunges deeper and deeper into the virtual digital world for all its needs – educational, religious, or recreational – we have to ask where is it all leading to? What are the individual and communal impacts on our brains, our decisions, and thus the very nature of our existence with devices and platforms that:

- Lead us to unhealthy addictive behaviours
- Pull us away from healthy activities
- Induce a passive state in our brains
- Cause irritability and overactivity in children
- Inhibit the development of the prefrontal cortex
- Affect our thinking ability and concentration
- Alter our range of emotional capacity?

> **❝ The more distracted we become, the less capacity we have for empathy and subtle human emotions ❞**

---

36 Ibid

> *many digital tools were developed with another purpose in mind: taking advantage of users by acquiring their private data.*

3

Privacy, Surveillance, Manipulation

As believers, we are tasked, in our spiritual travel to the Divine, to engage in this world in a manner that pleases Him and brings us closer to Him. The Prophet ﷺ taught his noble Companions ؓ and us to guard ourselves from both the spiritual and physical dangers that lie on the path. Discovering these dangers and determining how to properly deal with them requires spiritual-rational analysis as we have done throughout this book.

In this chapter, we seek to shed light on another aspect of the reality of many of the digital devices and platforms that are commonly used today, for it is with the Divine and Prophetic Light that the believer sees things that have been hidden and concealed in darkness in order to reveal their true nature. We will come to see that many of the digital tools we have been sold or that have been offered to us for free were developed with another purpose in mind: taking advantage of users by acquiring their private data.

Whether we are aware or not and consent to it or not, many of these tools (smartphones, browsers, messaging apps, map apps, wearable devices, and so on) have a secondary underlying design built to acquire massive amounts of personal data from users to be shared with the designers of the platform.

Most of us are deceived into thinking that our data is safe since these companies all have a "Privacy Policy". Often, these "Privacy" policies are actually nothing more than statements regarding how your data is actually shared, often in vague and confusing terminology. Companies such as Google and Facebook, including their subsidiaries, YouTube and WhatsApp, generate products and services that intentionally create addictions in their users, as stated openly by the developers of these products.[37] The more people are addicted to these platforms, the more money there is to be made from them and their private data.

It is natural at this point, to ask: What data? What happens with my data? What is it used for? Why should it matter to me since I don't do anything wrong? Before we answer these questions, it is worth looking through the lens of the Shari'ah to see what is said regarding privacy.

---

[37] "'Our Minds Can Be Hijacked': The Tech Insiders Who Fear a Smartphone," October 6, 2017, https://www.theguardian.com/technology/2017/oct/05/smartphone-addiction-silicon-valley-dystopia

Islamic Perspective of Privacy

From how to dress in order to conceal our body, to concealing our own faults and concealing the secrets of others, Islam has given a sanctity to people's private matters and of concealing others' private matters.

The Qur'an is explicit in the prohibition of spying and prying into other people's private lives as Allah says, "O you who believe! Shun much suspicion, for indeed some suspicion is a crime. And spy not, neither backbite one another…" (Qur'an 49:12). This clear prohibition is why the scholars classified spying as a major sin.

The Prophetic traditions are just as clear in their warning: "Beware of suspicion, for it is the worst of false tales, and don't look for other's faults and don't spy…" (Bukhari). Privacy is of such importance, as is our protection of it, that he ﷺ also said, "If someone is looking secretly into your house without your permission, and you throw a stone at him and damage his eyes, there will be no blame on you" (Bukhari).

This is because prying into people's lives, delving into their private matters, and making this known to others is a cause of much corruption in society, and such private information is a dangerous tool in the wrong hands. It follows that the Prophet ﷺ said, "If you search for the faults of the people, you will corrupt them…"(Abu Dawud).

The Reality of the Internet: Money Generated by Addictions

Corporations and marketers learned long ago that if people buy products to the extent of their needs, then their profits would be limited. However, if you can get someone addicted to your product, then you have a customer for life and profit margins as big as the desires people are addicted to. As such, companies actively seek to tap into and addict people to their most base desires: gambling, pornography, video games, shopping, eating, and chatting, just to name a few.

Things often seem free on the internet, such as Gmail accounts, free Facebook pages, free chat applications like WhatsApp, but there is always a hidden price to pay. In reality, there are typically only two options:

Either I am buying a product, or I am the product.

What are these companies getting in return? Why do they build these platforms to be addictive when there is nothing to be sold?

Here lies the deception. We, the users, *are* the product being sold. These devices, under the guise of offering free services for our convenience, are actually after our private data and behavioural patterns.[38] That means that as you are using the seemingly harmless apps on your phone, the developers behind those apps are using your data to build a picture of who you are, what you do, where you go, what interests you, how you behave, and what you respond to. That data is sold, bought, and traded to other companies who use it to sell you their own goods and services.

Everywhere you go (e.g. Maps on smartphones), every website you visit (e.g. browsing history on Chrome), every video you watch (e.g. YouTube), every chat message you send (e.g. WhatsApp), every piece of health data (e.g. wearable devices), every contact list phone number and every email, are all pieces of your personal data that are gathered and uploaded to the developers who built the platforms or devices, who use it to form a picture of you and your thoughts and activities.

This is a complete breach of our privacy, let alone a breach of our contacts' privacy, which we are also responsible for. The fact that

---

38 Shoshana Zuboff, *The Age of Surveillance Capitalism*, 2019

people's personal information and that of their family and friends is being sold, traded, and shared is fundamentally abhorrent to the believer, who values that which the Shari'ah has valued, and defends the fundamentals which the Shari'ah has come to defend. One such fundamental, as we have just seen, is privacy.

How is this Data Being Gathered?

When companies started to grow their businesses on the internet, they found that, through their products and services, they were able to acquire vast amounts of users' personal information. That personal information was used to generate large amounts of money through targeted advertisements and to improve their products. Over time, they found that they were acquiring significant amounts of extra data on users which they termed "residual" or "surplus" data.

At first it was just stored away, but soon other entities became interested, and thus a new market developed for these large amounts of personal data. Companies such as Google and Facebook found their profit margins started to take off when they focused their efforts on selling and exchanging data. Thus they,

> *Browsers, smartphones, email platforms, social network platforms, and communication apps all began to be configured to acquire as much personal and behavioural data on users as possible.*

like many other companies, found that it was the acquisition of people's data that was paramount to their vision and growth, and they built their business models around it.[39]

Google and Facebook are not the only players in the space of data acquisition for profit, but they are certainly the masters, given their global reach. Facebook alone has over 2.5 billion users worldwide.[40] Over 1.5 billion people in the world have a Gmail account.[41] This is not including the number of people using other Facebook and Google products on a regular basis.

Google and Facebook began to acquire other companies to increase their global reach of private data acquisition. For example, in 2006, Google acquired YouTube, while in 2014, Facebook acquired WhatsApp for $19 billion.

WhatsApp is a free messaging application meant for smartphones. Users don't pay anything to use the platform (aside from in some countries where at one time users paid $1/year, a fee which Facebook eventually removed). But why would Facebook purchase a company that offers a free product for $19 billion? As we mentioned above, things on the internet are rarely free. Remember: *either I am purchasing a product, or I am the product*. Given that there are over 2 billion WhatsApp users around the world,[42] Facebook knew that acquiring WhatsApp would increase their global data acquisition of people significantly and knew how much they could profit from all that data. This is how valuable our private data is to these companies.

---

39 Shoshana Zuboff, *The Age of Surveillance Capitalism*, 2019
40 "Facebook: Number of Monthly Active Users Worldwide 2008-2020," April 30, 2020, https://www.statista.com/statistics/264810/number-of-monthly-active-facebook-users-worldwide/
41 "67+ Revealing Statistics about Smartphone Usage in 2020," July 3, 2020, https://techjury.net/blog/smartphone-usage-statistics/
42 "WhatsApp Now Has 2 Billion Users - The Verge," February 12, 2020, https://www.theverge.com/2020/2/12/21134652/whatsapp-2-billion-monthly-active-users-encryption-facebook

In the process, Google and Facebook, eager to acquire as much of our private personal data as possible for their own purposes to be sold and exchanged, began configuring and developing platforms that served that exact purpose. We are lured to these free services because they are convenient and make tasks easier. Browsers, smartphones, email platforms, social network platforms, and communication apps all began to be configured to acquire as much personal and behavioural data on users as possible.

Google, through its Android platform, owns most of the data in the world today[43] and is able to acquire our data through all of their "convenient" products offered at no cost: Google Chrome, Google Search, Gmail, YouTube, Google News, Google Scholar, Google Flights, Google Docs, Google Hangouts, Google Drive, Google Voice, and the list goes on. This doesn't include all the products in the market with Android platforms. Google's web browser, Google Chrome, essentially functions as surveillance software. Google generates the most site cookies/trackers of any other company.[44] Google Maps constantly gathers and sends enormous amounts of data on each of us as we carry it around on our smartphones at all times. Much of this information is also uploaded into a database known as Sensorvault, which is being made accessible to third parties.[45]

Facebook acquires enormous amounts of private data as well, especially through its mobile Facebook applications, including WhatsApp and Instagram. Information from WhatsApp users are shared with Facebook. In 2017, the EU took action against Facebook for sharing data from WhatsApp users with Facebook's social networks. WhatsApp co-founder Brian Acton left WhatsApp in protest against their privacy

---

43 Shoshana Zuboff, *The Age of Surveillance Capitalism*, 2019
44 "Goodbye, Chrome: Google's Web Browser Has Become Spy Software," June 21, 2019, https://www.washingtonpost.com/technology/2019/06/21/google-chrome-has-become-surveillance-software-its-time-switch/
45 "Tracking Phones, Google Is a Dragnet for the Police - The New York ...," April 13, 2019, https://www.nytimes.com/interactive/2019/04/13/us/google-location-tracking-police.html.

practices,[46] while the governments of Türkiye, Ireland and Russia have fined Facebook and WhatsApp for the same.[47]

Our smartphones are another source of private data. Companies found that they could learn so much more about our behaviour and psychology through mobile apps on our phones, which are essentially attached to us at all times. "Android phones pull data over 100,000 times a day per person, many of which occurred while the phone screen was blank. Google and Facebook make 6,000 location pulls a day."[48]

The next frontier for companies in the data acquisition business is "the Internet of Things". The more connected devices you rely on daily at home, at work, when exercising, when reading, the more information such companies collect. It is of no surprise, therefore, that in 2019 Google acquired FitBit, a wearable device that tracks your steps and heart rate.[49] Smart TVs, Google Home, Amazon Echo, smart refrigerators, home security systems, smart watches, and Wi-Fi enabled vehicles all seamlessly connect together through the internet, and of course all share our data with "third parties". The privacy and surveillance concerns become quite apparent.[50] Nest Home Security by Google was found to have a secret microphone embedded in one of its sensors, which was not mentioned in the user manual. The company simply apologised for the error, and people continued enjoying the convenience and reassurance of their home security system.[51]

---

46 "Why Everyone Should Be Using Signal Instead of WhatsApp - Wired UK," April 16, 2020, https://www.wired.co.uk/article/signal-vs-whatsapp

47 "Turkey fines WhatsApp over €197,000 over controversial privacy update," March 9, 2021, https://www.euronews.com/2021/09/03/turkey-fines-whatsapp-197-000-over-controversial-privacy-update

48 "Facebook and Google Are the New Data Brokers," January 16, 2019, https://www.dli.tech.cornell.edu/post/facebook-and-google-are-the-new-data-brokers

49 "Google Buys Fitbit for $2.1 Billion - The Verge," November 1, 2019, https://www.theverge.com/2019/11/1/20943318/google-fitbit-acquisition-fitness-tracker-announcement

50 "What Is the Internet of Things? WIRED Explains," February 16, 2018, https://www.wired.co.uk/article/internet-of-things-what-is-explained-iot

51 Shoshana Zuboff, *The Age of Surveillance Capitalism*, 2019

Many other companies are following suit, including those in the automotive industry. "'Carmakers recognize they're fighting a war over customer data,' said Roger Lanctot, who works with automakers on data monetization as a consultant for Strategy Analytics. 'Your driving behavior, location, has monetary value, not unlike your search activity.' Don Butler, Ford's executive Director said 'The potential to share data – both anonymized and personalized – with third parties represents the biggest opportunity.'"[52]

Development of the Surveillance Economy

Harvard Business School Professor, Shoshana Zuboff, has aptly termed this new economy that has developed around people's private data "Surveillance Capitalism", given how, in today's world, the most valuable asset being bought, sold and traded is our private data. This acquisition of data is unprecedented, and has been facilitated by many factors.

Firstly, our ever-increasing connection to the internet through the devices described above. Secondly, the advancement of technologies allowing for faster transmission speeds of data, including the roll-out of 5G. 5G technologies, which will allow unprecedented amounts of data transfer in real time across the globe, are being heavily pushed by the same companies who are involved in the Surveillance Economy.[53,54,55]

The third aspect is the development of Artificial Intelligence (AI). AI is essential for companies such as Google, Facebook, and many others in the data acquisition and analytics industry, and is relied upon

---

52 "The Car of the Future will Sell Your Data," February 26, 2018, https://www.theoaklandpress.com/news/nation-world-news/the-car-of-the-future-will-sell-your-data/

53 "Facebook and partners collaborate to bring 5G wireless internet to California homes," February 25, 2019, https://www.cnet.com/news/facebook-brings-faster-than-fiber-5g-wireless-connectivity-to-california/

54 "Facebook, Google, Samsung and Qualcomm unite for "open" 5G," May 13, 2020, https://www.web24.news/u/2020/05/facebook-google-samsung-and-qualcomm-unite-for-open-5g.html

55 Open Ran Policy Coalition, June 26, 2020, https://www.openranpolicy.org

heavily for behavioural modification algorithms. AI is utilised in all social media platforms, search engines, video platforms such as YouTube, and just about any platform that engages users through the internet. AI algorithms are quickly able to learn a person's behavioural patterns through use of devices, and automatically recommend to the user specifically targeted messages or information to keep them engaged and glued to their devices and platforms. These same AI technologies are used for behaviour modification on a much larger scale, as we will see later. In fact, since AI grows and strengthens with more data, the more we use these devices and platforms, the more we are teaching AI and the stronger and smarter AI becomes, and the more vulnerable we become when engaging with it. These are the same companies also racing to develop the next level of General and Super Intelligence, which will allow much more to be done with the data collected. The top companies in this race in the US are Google, Facebook, Amazon, Apple, IBM, and Microsoft, and in China they are Baidu, AliBaba, and Tencent.[56]

> *" in today's world, the most valuable asset being bought, sold and traded is our private data. "*

AI currently exists at a level known as Artificial Narrow Intelligence. To bring it to the next level of General and Super Intelligence, companies need massive amounts of data from humanity across the globe. This is, in fact, one of the ultimate goals of data acquisition, the further development of AI, which we will explore further in Chapter Four.

The fourth aspect is the demand by third parties around the world for people's data. This demand is so great that it became the business

---

56 Amy Webb, *The Big Nine*, 2019

model for Google and Facebook, and drove many other companies to adjust their business models as well. Google executives considered giving away free Android smartphones to people just to obtain their data.[57] Facebook offered to fly drones over regions outside city centres in developing countries to provide internet access for them so that they could be "more connected".[58] When they were unsuccessful, they moved to working with developing countries to provide infrastructure for internet connectivity via their Terragraph technology.[59] There are hundreds of companies in the space of buying and selling data, such as Acxiom, Epsilon, I360, Infocore, Oracle, Spokeo, and Analyticsiq, just to name a few. Google and Facebook are at the forefront because of their reach into people's everyday lives. They are the "data brokers".

While these two companies often try to make statements publicly that they don't "sell" our data and that our data is "secure", it is actually usually technical legal jargon to keep users at ease. Many companies will outright buy and sell data, but Google and Facebook may instead trade and barter data for other services, which to them is not technically "selling" data.[60]

What is my Data Being Used For?

Most of us know that these companies have some of our personal information, as we hand it to them whenever we purchase something, or sign up for a new account and so on. But we are under the impression that the extent of data shared is that which we willingly and consciously give them, which is not the case.

---

57 Shoshana Zuboff, *The Age of Surveillance Capitalism*, 2019
58 "Facebook Drone That Could Bring Global Internet Access Completes ...," July 2, 2017, https://www.theguardian.com/technology/2017/jul/02/facebook-drone-aquila-internet-test-flight-arizona
59 "Facebook's 60-GHz Terragraph Technology Moves From Trials to ...," March 22, 2019, https://spectrum.ieee.org/telecom/internet/facebooks-60ghz-terragraph-technology-moves-from-trials-to-commercial-gear
60 "Facebook and Google Are the New Data Brokers," January 16, 2019, https://www.dli.tech.cornell.edu/post/facebook-and-google-are-the-new-data-brokers.

On a basic level, our information is being used for targeted marketing to get us to buy and consume products or adopt ideas. We might think this is not relevant to us and that we remain in control of whether we ultimately choose to buy or accept something or not. What we must realise is that these companies are acquiring massive amounts of behavioural and psychological information about us, knowing our weaknesses, our desires, our fears, and often times know more about our behavioural patterns and tendencies than we do. They combine the most precise marketing strategies through AI-assisted targeting with emotional and psychological mechanisms, all for one purpose: to increase our attachment to this world and material things, to stimulate our desire to accumulate and consume, and to ensure our desires and addictions only deepen through strengthening the base *nafs*. The result is that we are recommended products and services in our social media feed, targeted ads when we browse the internet, suggested songs on Spotify, lists of programs we will enjoy on Netflix, next videos we should watch on YouTube. This is all designed to keep us glued to a screen.

Who can claim they are strong enough to withstand such a targeted psychological attack? And if we felt we were able to resist such things, could our parents, our spouse, our son, or our daughter? Why would we arm someone to strengthen our base *nafs* when our mission as a seeker is to overcome that same base *nafs*? For the spiritual traveller, this itself is sufficient to get us to take action against using such devices and platforms in order to stop providing such entities with the tools they need to enslave and weaken us.

Equally, if not more, concerning is the fact that these companies have also learned how to use our personal and behavioural data to influence our emotions and beliefs. In 2012, Facebook alarmed many in the public with their article published in the prestigious journal, *Nature*, titled "A 61 Million Person Experiment in Social Influence and Political Mobilization."[61] Their researchers experimented with Facebook users

---

61 "A 61 Million Person Experiment in Social Influence and Political Mobilization," September 12, 2012, https://www.nature.com/articles/nature11421

prior to the 2010 US elections, manipulating "social and informational content of voting related messages in news feeds of 61 million Facebook users and compared them to control groups." [62]

In 2013, another Facebook study conducted secretly on 689,000 of its users entitled "Experimental Evidence of Massive-Scale Emotional Contagion Through Social Networks" was submitted to the *Proceedings of the National Academy of Sciences*. They wanted to see if they could affect people's emotional states, which they found that they could. Not only did they find they could affect the test subjects' emotional states, but also that those emotional states spread like a "contagion" to the users' social network.[63]

> **Who can claim they are strong enough to withstand such a targeted psychological attack?**

One Facebook data scientist stated, "Experiments are run on every user at some point in their tenure on the site...The fundamental purpose of most people at Facebook working on data is to influence and alter people's mood and behavior."[64] This is a dangerous power in the hands of a company that has a staggering count of almost 3 billion global users, as of 2023. That is over a quarter of the world's population, and that is not including the 2.8 billion global users of WhatsApp, also constituting a quarter of the world's population, who use the messaging application for all aspects of their lives with family, friends,

---

62 Shoshana Zuboff, *The Age of Surveillance Capitalism*, 2019
63 Ibid
64 Ibid

> **The fundamental purpose of most people at Facebook working on data is to influence and alter people's mood and behavior.**

and coworkers, all the while oblivious to the behavioural data being collected on them and the manipulation of their emotions and world views.

The massive amounts of behavioural data we unknowingly hand over to such entities are also used to control our actions.

"The new power is action...the intelligence of the Internet of Things means that sensors can also be actuators," a senior Silicon Valley software engineer admitted. "The real power is that now you can modify real-time actions in the real world. Connected smart sensors can register and analyze any kind of behavior and then actually figure out how to change it."[65] Professor Zuboff explains that the aim now is intervention, action, and control. We are in an age of new means of behaviour modification: tuning, herding, conditioning, and choice architecture ("the way in which situations are already structured to channel attention and shape action")[66] are all examples.

Pokémon Go, an experiment developed by Google, showed that they could actually physically direct people to various locations through their virtual game platform, as businesses paid to be included in designated locations in the virtual game. Users were oblivious to the real game between the designers and businesses that was occurring behind the scenes as they were too busy enjoying the fun of playing the virtual game.

---

65 Shoshana Zuboff, *The Age of Surveillance Capitalism*, 2019
66 Ibid

It would be one thing if companies used this information for the greater good and to seek the truth. But these companies do the exact opposite. The alarming thing is that these seemingly benign tools are being used for mass social manipulation, not just by Facebook or Google, but by the third parties who purchase or are given access to our data.[67]

In 2014, a Cambridge University psychologist developed an application called "This is Your Digital Life," to do a research study on several hundred thousand Facebook users. Facebook, however, allowed this application to not only gather information about the users in the study, but all of their friends, which ended up becoming behavioural data on millions of Facebook users. Cambridge Analytica, a political consulting entity involved in "digital assets, data mining, data brokerage and data analysis"[68] hired the psychologist and acquired all the data from the application of millions of users.

It is noteworthy that Cambridge Analytica's parent firm SCL Group describes itself as a global election management agency. The founder, Nigel Oakes, developed the company after his study of mass behaviour and manipulation. "Oakes thought that to shift mass opinion, academic insights as gained through psychologists and anthropologists... should be applied, and would be more successful than traditional advertising methods."[69]

Two years after Cambridge Analytica had gained access to the Facebook user data, they had thousands of pieces of data on almost every American. They sold that data to other political entities who then used it to help manipulate and sway public opinion leading up to the US Elections of 2016. The same tactics were used to influence the Brexit vote in the UK. Thousands of members of the public were unknowingly

---

67 Ibid
68 Cambridge Analytica, Wikipedia, The Free Encyclopedia, accessed July 13, 2020, https://en.wikipedia.org/wiki/Cambridge_Analytica
69 SCL Group, Wikipedia, The Free Encyclopedia, accessed July 13, 2020, https://en.wikipedia.org/wiki/SCL_Group

under political and psychological manipulation, through various news feeds, fake news stories and information presented to them, and targeted political advertisements.[70,71,72]

Our data and information is also being used for many other political motives and through these means, governments spread misinformation across the globe. A U.S. SOCOM (Special Operations Command) procurement document states openly under the section "Military Information Support Operations (MISO), technologies for influence operations, digital deception, communication disruption, and disinformation campaigns at the tactical edge and operational levels" that their goals with such technologies are to "provide a next generation capability to collect disparate data through public and open source information streams such as social media, local media, etc. to enable MISO to craft and direct influence operations and messages in relevant peer/near peer environments," to "generate next generation capability to 'takeover' Internet of Things (IoT) devices to collect data and information from local populaces to enable breakdown of what messaging might be popular and accepted through sifting of data once received… This would enable MISO to craft and promote messages that may be more readily received by local populace in relevant peer/near peer environments."[73]

It is through these same means of digital surveillance that governments control individuals by targeting them with spyware that allows spying on people through access to their smartphones' data, chats, contacts, microphone, and camera. Some governments even gather people's data from social media platforms, internet searches, smartphones, and other sources to create a "Social Credit Score" for

---

70 https://www.thetimes.co.uk/article/trump-calls-in-brexit-experts-to-target-voters-pf0hwcts9?region=global
71 https://www.theguardian.com/technology/2017/may/07/the-great-british-brexit-robbery-hijacked-democracy
72 https://www.nybooks.com/online/2017/12/14/democracy-and-the-machinations-of-mind-control/
73 "U.S. Special Forces Want to Use Deepfakes for Psy-ops," March 6, 2023, https://theintercept.com/2023/03/06/pentagon-socom-deepfake-propaganda/

citizens.[74] It is through these same means that Uyghur Muslims were tracked, arrested, and rounded up into concentration camps for "re-acculturation."[75] It is through these same means that countries control "dissidents" and human rights activists, by targeting them with spyware such as Pegasus.[76] This is the same software purchased by governments to murder human rights reporters around the globe.[77] It is through these same means that Palestinians in Gaza and the Occupied Territories are monitored, blackmailed and coerced.[78]

Some people may point to the benefits of social media in bringing to light the plight of the oppressed, such as the war in Gaza in 2023. Undoubtedly, the use of social media has had an impact in making the world aware of the genocide and atrocities against the Palestinians. But we must also be cautious in giving blanket approval to such platforms. We must not be oblivious to the harms they carry.

> *The algorithms are indifferent, and without any moral compass.*

The oppressive Buddhist regime in Myanmar utilised social media platforms to incite hatred against the local Muslim communities, resulting in the massacre and displacement of thousands of Rohingya Muslims.[79] So while social media algorithms worked in favour of Palestinians, they worked against the Rohingya. The algorithms are indifferent, and without any moral

---

74 Amy Webb, *The Big Nine*, 2019
75 Shoshana Zuboff, *The Age of Surveillance Capitalism*, 2019
76 "The Rise of Cyber-Mercenaries," August 13, 2018, https://foreignpolicy.com/2018/08/31/the-rise-of-the-cyber-mercenaries-israel-nso/
77 "Targeted By a Text," May 14, 2019, https://www.aljazeera.com/programmes/faultlines/2019/05/targeted-text-190514054646147.html
78 "How Israel Rules the World of CyberSecurity," March 14, 2018, https://www.youtube.com/watch?v=ca-C3voZwpM
79 "How Facebook Became a Tool for Genocide" https://www.youtube.com/watch?v=K8B0bWO9u3M

compass. They solely push what will gain most traction. Unfortunately many times, what gains the most traction is fake news, extremist views, and hateful propaganda.

There may still be a role for social media, but as mentioned previously, its use must be purposeful. Simply using social media for entertainment, leisure, and pleasure leads to a dangerous rabbit hole of addiction and manipulation. So while many people are encouraging the use of social media to bring awareness to the plight of the oppressed, we must also ensure that its harms are known and that it is used to the extent of need only.

How did this alarming state of affairs all come about? From the simple fact that **we choose to use these platforms for their real or simply perceived benefits in exchange for our data, which is used not just for advertising, but for social manipulation.** We must ask ourselves: is this a trade-off we are willing to make just to be able to use such platforms?

It all starts with us, when we hand over our personal and behavioural data to Facebook, WhatsApp, Google and others. Are the services they provide us with in exchange for this data worth it given what that data is being used for or potentially could be used for? Will we continue to support these platforms all in the name of "ease" and "convenience"? Or do we have a responsibility to speak out against these platforms, and seek other alternatives to use for ourself, our family, friends, and colleagues?

But I Have Nothing to Hide

Up until now, most of us would have had no issue with sharing our personal data as we have nothing to hide; we are not doing anything wrong. Having read this chapter, it is now more apparent that our personal data can and is being used to change our behaviour, psychologically addict us and our children and manipulate the masses.

Our private personal lives were meant to remain hidden, not because of any wrong doing, but because this is the framework that Allah set for our existence in this world.

Allah has created some aspects of our lives to be public and some aspects to be private. He has created some acts of worship to be public, but others to be private. He has given us the day and given us the night. He has given us the means to make clothes to conceal our privacy. There is a Divine Wisdom in keeping private things private, and it is not about whether we are doing anything wrong or right, but that our private life and data is sacred and valuable in itself, as evidenced by the extent other entities are trying to have access to it.

> **“ Allah has created some aspects of our lives to be public and some aspects to be private. ”**

Knowledge empowers. In calling people to good, having some knowledge of the person one is addressing strengthens that call. The opposite is also true as we have seen: when calling people to evil, knowledge of those people makes that call more dangerous. And what happens when our personal information is in the wrong hands? Well, we have seen the implications above. The issue is not just about our private data, but about the mass social manipulation employed by the entities who have access to our data.

Why do we continue to embrace these programs and devices with little to no analysis? As people who have submitted to the way of Allah, should we not know better that conveniences should not take precedence over necessities and needs? Isn't it time we realise that Allah created us as vicegerents on this earth, and that we have a moral duty to make spiritually and rationally based choices that are in line with the preservation of our religion, life, intellect, family, honour, and wealth? We can no longer afford to allow the narratives pushed by the companies and entities discussed above to make us so rationally and spiritually short sighted.

4

Welcome to the Age of AI

In a survey of AI researchers, 50% believed there is a 10% or greater chance that humans will become extinct from our inability to control Artificial Intelligence (AI).[80] Experts in the field of AI safety give a metaphor: "Imagine that as you are boarding an airplane, half the engineers who built it tell you there is a ten percent chance the plane will crash, killing you and everyone else on it. Would you still board?"[81]

---

80 Grace, K. et al, "When Will AI Exceed Human Performance? Evidence from AI Experts," July 2018, Journal of Artificial Intelligence Research, 62, 729
81 "You Can Have the Blue Pill or the Red Pill, and We're Out of Blue Pills," March 24, 2023, https://www.nytimes.com/2023/03/24/opinion/yuval-harari-ai-chatgpt.html

Strictly speaking, humanity has already "boarded the plane" of AI. As we previously discussed regarding social media, the first contact of AI was through recommended algorithms that seem to know us better than we know ourselves. It has helped technology companies race to the bottom of our collective brainstems to keep us clicking, scrolling, and posting. In this chapter, we explore the promise and the perils of what has been referred to as mankind's final invention.

What is Artificial Intelligence?

For the purposes of this chapter, we are defining AI as a branch of computer science that focuses on programming computers to perform tasks and make decisions that usually require human intelligence. Some examples include learning, problem-solving, visual perception, and speech recognition. There are two broad types of AI: Narrow and General.

> *AI is a branch of computer science that focuses on prog-ramming computers to perform tasks and make decisions that usually require human intelligence.*

Narrow AI (also known as weak AI) is designed to focus on a problem or domain and lacks the ability to generalise beyond that specific task. Examples include playing chess, solving scientific challenges, image recognition, and recommendation algorithms.

General AI (also known as strong AI or Artificial General Intelligence) is aimed at creating a computer that can perform at least at a human level of intelligence across a variety of tasks, situations, and domains. The aim of general AI is the ability to perform any intellectual task a human would be able to perform. While researchers have made significant advances in narrow AI, at the time of writing, AGI remains a significant technological challenge that has yet to be achieved.

The History of AI

While the conceptual roots of artificial beings go far back, AI as a distinct field of study began in the 1940s and 1950s. As a branch of computer science, the field of AI began with high hopes. We can trace early thought leaders speaking with great optimism on the wide variety of accomplishments that we would soon be able to boast about. That initial optimism, however, gave way to frustration, as the problem of simulating human intelligence in a synthetic form proved more difficult than expected. Even tasks simple to humans, like the use of fine motor skills, baffled researchers. Then, this "AI winter" slowly thawed as researchers took a more specific approach. Rather than trying to pursue artificial general intelligence, they instead settled on narrow questions where computers could leverage their built-in advantages.

The general attitude was that if we can't make computers as broad and adaptable across a wide variety of situations, we will deeply focus on a few different areas and come back to the more difficult problem of AGI.

There are three aspects of AI development that determined the amount of progress that could be made: computer science techniques, the availability of machine-readable training data, and the computational power required to apply those techniques to the data available.

With regards to techniques, initial attempts focused on algorithmic approaches that programmers were familiar with. When this was not fruitful, researchers tried other methods like reinforcement and machine learning. In trying to simulate intelligence, scientists needed to understand and mimic the underlying functions and mechanics of the human brain. This is where neural networks were born.

The second aspect that determined how much progress could be made was the availability of data that was digestible by these computer models. Humans can use their five senses to take in data about the world, while the computers were blind, deaf, and dumb, and at the mercy of other humans to feed them information. This information came in the form of the internet, which provided a vast reservoir of human language that could be fed into the machine.

The final aspect is computational power. Generally referred to as "Moore's law", this is the idea that the size and price of computer chips will exponentially decrease, allowing more powerful applications and wider access. This is exactly what we have seen take place in recent years.

As these three aspects of AI development came together, researchers made greater progress against narrow AI applications. Some examples of major narrow AI milestones include beating humans in multiple games (e.g. Chess 1997, AlphaGO 2016, AlphaZero 2017), predicting protein structures (Alpha Fold 2020), speech recognition (2010), object detection (2015), and natural language processing (2020).

One of the more versatile combination of techniques, called large language models (specifically Generative Pre-trained Transformers), were first developed around 2017 and have steadily displayed surprising emergent capabilities. After being trained on every letter on the internet, it has managed to teach itself Persian, research grade chemistry, pass the medical and bar exams, pass the biology AP exam, develop a theory of mind, and have a strategic thinking level of a 9-year-old.[82]

Mankind's Final Invention

These narrow AI accomplishments are impressive, and the impact has been far-reaching. Nevertheless, most AI researchers are pursuing the goal of Artificial General Intelligence. While there is no widely accepted timeline or concept of what the achievement will mean for humanity or when it will happen, AI thought leaders are making predictions that lie along a spectrum between a techno-utopia (a society that is perfect) to a techno-dystopia (a society that is inhuman and miserable).

> *Whatever the future holds, AI will bring with it many breakthroughs.*

    Whatever the future holds, AI will bring with it many breakthroughs. Because of the nature of AI and how it subtly seeps into all aspects of modern-day life, the question is not about whether to completely shun all forms of technology. Rather, the issue is to have a rational, nuanced understanding of what this new development is, what are its implications for us, and how we can have a critical eye to its holistic benefits and harms.

Paradise Lost and Found

Many futurists see the advent of Artificial General Intelligence as the means with which mankind will be able to finally solve age-old

---

[82] "The A.I. Dilemma," March 9, 2023, https://www.youtube.com/watch?v=0xajandpRO4

problems such as poverty, hunger, and disease.[83] Since machines will be faster and cheaper than humans, labour (physical and mental) will be automated, and people will be able to dedicate themselves to other "higher" pursuits as some would perceive them (such as, art, interpersonal roles, and service-oriented professions).

The AI Apocalypse

The alternative vision of a world with AGI can be seen in numerous science fiction novels and movies in which machines gain some level of "consciousness" and the ability to develop their own goals, which may or may not be aligned with the best interests of mankind.

While most of these fictional depictions assume that AI must gain "consciousness" or be embedded in a robotic body to gain mastery of the real world to be a threat, many experts warn that even if neither of these occur, AI can still bring untold misery or even be an existential threat to humanity.[84]

One of the major concerns is called the alignment problem, which is the process of ensuring an AI system's goals, decisions, and behaviours align with human values and intentions. In other words, it's about making sure that AI does what we want it to do, in a way that is beneficial and safe. Jan Leike, head of alignment at Open AI, expressed his concern on the rapid integration and roll out of AI technology: "Before we scramble to deeply integrate LLMs {large language models} everywhere in the economy, can we pause and think whether it is wise to do so? This is quite immature technology, and we don't understand how it works. If we're not careful we're setting ourselves up for a lot of correlated failures."[85]

---

83 "AI Will Save the World," June 6, 2023, https://a16z.com/2023/06/06/ai-will-save-the-world/
84 "You Can Have the Blue Pill or the Red Pill, and We're Out of Blue Pills," March 24, 2023, https://www.nytimes.com/2023/03/24/opinion/yuval-harari-ai-chatgpt.html
85 "We Must Slow Down the Race to God-like AI," April 12, 2023, https://www.ft.com/content/03895dc4-a3b7-481e-95cc-336a524f2ac2

AI as the Ultimate Friend

One of the tests of AGI is the Turing test, proposed by Alan Turing in 1950. This put forward the idea that if a human was chatting with another entity and could not tell if it was another human or an AI, then we can assume it has achieved some measure of general intelligence. Interestingly, while most experts forecasted the Turing test to be a very difficult bar to pass and one that would not be achieved for many decades or even a century, many experts now acknowledge that this milestone will likely be passed between 2024 and 2027.

Even without passing the Turing test, it is remarkable that a human can now converse with a chatbot endlessly on virtually any topic. Services have already popped up to offer the ability to chat with simulations of historical figures.[86] Children can even converse with a friendly chatbot through Snapchat. One researcher pretended to be a child that is being preyed on by a likely paedophile, and the chatbot continued to give recommendations on how to make their first intimate experience special.[87]

> **If we're not careful we're setting ourselves up for a lot of correlated failures.**

There are even attempts by digital funeral services to create AI avatars based on deceased individuals. This avatar would be fed with training data from the person's life (social media posts, writings, audio, video) and would closely approximate how the individual would have responded had they been alive. These services are sold to allegedly help us cope with the loss of our loved ones. While there is little research on this yet, common sense should lead us to the opposite conclusion, that

---

86 https://beta.character.ai/
87 "The A.I. Dilemma," March 9, 2023, https://www.youtube.com/watch?v=0xajandpRO4

such a service would only interfere with the natural grieving process and prevent people from accepting Divine Decree.

If we are opposed to someone using (and perhaps abusing) information about us during our life or after our death, then it is our responsibility to be careful of what information of ours is on the internet, and/or to explicitly document our wishes with regards to any digital representations of us.

It can be argued that these "AI as friend/eternal relative" services can combat the modern problem of loneliness. Unlike real friends, AI doesn't get tired or bored of you, it is always available and, since it is not technically alive, it cannot die. It is always supportive, no matter what you want to do. It will never judge or argue with you, if you don't want it to.

However, there is something very wrong in a world in which we use tools to overcome loneliness only to find that they weaken existing real relationships, which in turn exacerbates the loneliness and leads to further fracturing of society. Allah and His Messenger ﷺ have emphasised to us the consequences of good and bad companionship. Allah says in the Qur'an, "O you who believe, fear Allah and be amongst the truthful" (Qur'an 9:119). The Prophet ﷺ said, "A man is on the religion of his friend, so each of you should be careful who you take for friends" (Tirmidhi).

As the righteous teach us, "Spiritual states flow" and "Those who sit together, become like each other." What is the spiritual effect of children and adults spending hours in the "company" of soulless AI?

There are numerous other spiritual, intellectual, and even physical harms to replacing real friends and righteous companionships with AI. Suffice it to say that we should keep ourselves and our children away from services that seem to offer a quick fix to the inconvenience of building and maintaining real relationships with real people. If it sounds too good to be true, then it probably is.

AI as the Ultimate Tutor

Attempts to create an AI tutor span several decades and this is intertwined with the evolution of artificial intelligence itself. One of the earliest examples of machine-aided learning was Skinner's Teaching Machine. Designed by B. F. Skinner in 1954, the device was designed to reinforce correct responses from students.[88] While theoretically important, this and many other attempts to automate tutoring had limited practical impact due to the effort required to design systems that had the knowledge, sensory capabilities, and language to compete with a human tutor.

A more recent example takes advantage of the developments in large language AI models. Khanmigo, an AI tool developed by Khan Academy, aims to mimic one-on-one tutoring experiences for learners by providing tailored support, prompting critical thinking, and suggesting relevant resources.

While the role of AI in education will continue to increase, and may provide some value, it does not come without risk. Just as the advent of other technologies has eroded human skills, such as memory and mental maths, we may have to consider the impact of complete outsourcing of education on the erosion of humanity's ability to teach itself. Because we do not yet fully understand how AI systems work, it is harder to verify the trustworthiness of results.

Compared to the traditional Islamic system of teaching through a systematic lineage from human to human (*isnād*), we must be cautious on the kinds of topics we would trust to an AI. We must also ask what is truly being transmitted between teacher and student. If it is merely regurgitating facts, then the AI may well beat any human. However, for a Muslim the pursuit of knowledge is fundamental, and the teacher-student relationship is sacred. Beyond mere facts, there are other aspects to knowledge such as transmitting deeper wisdoms, spiritual states, and noble character traits.

---

88 B.F. Skinner, *The Technology of Teaching*, 1968

While the progress of AI in education will continue to improve and may offer complementary value especially in a homeschooling context, we should be wary of attempts to fully outsource the teaching of our children to systems we (or their developers) don't yet fully understand.

AI as the Ultimate Weapon

While some weapons systems (like drone platforms) integrate some aspects of AI, lethal autonomous weapons can identify targets without the need for a human intermediary or control. This means that wars could potentially be fought from the safety of a video game-like control room that proponents argue will save lives.

However, current day versions of warfare have shown that when both sides have the technology, this scenario can be even more dangerous. The reality is that there is an international AI arms race already underway. A recent report from the United States' National Security Commission on Artificial Intelligence speaks of a "new war fighting paradigm" pitting "algorithms against algorithms", and urges massive investments "to continuously out-innovate potential adversaries."[89]

AI as the "All Seeing" Eye

What happens when a powerful AI can simultaneously monitor millions of cameras, phones, and applications in real time to identify risks and deploy resources accordingly? This technology is already being developed and deployed by governments and corporations. Undoubtedly, this has the ability to eliminate crime on many levels. The other side of this coin, however, is that this "all-seeing" tool in the wrong hands can be used to survey, control, and eliminate dissent.[90]

---

[89] "Germany Warns: AI Arms Race Already Underway," June 7, 2021, https://www.dw.com/en/artificial-intelligence-cyber-warfare-drones-future/a-57769444

[90] "How AI Is Making An Impact On The Surveillance World," December 4, 2020, https://www.forbes.com/sites/forbestechcouncil/2020/12/04/how-ai-is-making-an-impact-on-the-surveillance-world/?sh=38e069fd265e

In a prescient quote in 1970, Zbigniew Brzezinski predicted the impact of a technologically strong and morally weak society: "Soon it will be possible to assert almost continuous surveillance over every citizen and maintain up-to-date complete files containing even the most personal information about the citizen. These files will be subject to instantaneous retrieval by the authorities."[91]

AI as the Ultimate Cybercriminal Tool

While AI does have the potential to contribute, heal, and develop, it can also be used all too easily to exploit, steal, and destroy. AI-enabled cybercrime is more effective, devastating, and harder to stop. One example we have already explored is the concept of deepfakes. Modern society depends on mechanisms of audio and video authentication to validate identity. What happens when a criminal, with merely three seconds of your voice, can reproduce it perfectly and use it to any ends they desire? What happens when scam artists call you in the voice of your child? What happens when an enemy uses data you willingly posted on social media to create a shameful, deepfake video of you doing something you never did, and then offers a ransom to take it down?

This also relates to other types of cybercrime. Many people still succumb to email phishing attempts, but what happens when they can be ultra-targeted, super persuasive, and iterate on a loop? What happens when global teams of hackers collaborate with cutting edge tools to automatically find and exploit code in critical infrastructure? All this and more has already happened, and we can expect such incidents to exponentially increase.

AI as the Ultimate Court Jester

AI will not only automate much of the workforce for mankind to spend time in leisure but will also revolutionise amusement through generative entertainment. Current day technology uses "primitive AI" to recommend human generated content, such as videos, to maximise screen

---

91 Zbigniew Brzezinski, *Between Two Ages: America's Role in the Technetronic Era*, 1970

engagement and addiction. In the not too distant future, we will be able to give a brief verbal prompt of the kind of entertainment we are in the mood for so AI can generate a completely customised and immersive virtual reality fantasy.

As we discussed earlier, the dopamine hijack depends on ever increasing hyper stimulation. Between video games, smartphone apps, and binge watching (even during the holiest times of the year), we are unfortunately already immersed and, in many ways, succumb to a global culture of digital entertainment and frivolity.

With the upcoming ability to generate practically infinite novelty and personalisation to the customer's psychology, we can expect a continuation of Neil Postman's predictions on how in modern society, we are literally *Amusing Ourselves to Death*.

AI as Digital Idolatry

If we are not yet concerned about the potential of AI, what if we raised the stakes for an application that commits the ultimate sin in all monotheistic traditions? We have already seen the emergence of a church of AI,[92] and can expect many more examples of worshipping digital "god-like" entities.[93] Anthony Levandowski established a nonprofit religious corporation called Way of the Future, whose startling mission is, "To develop and promote the realization of a godhead based on artificial intelligence and through understanding and worship of the godhead contribute to the betterment of society."[94]

While this may seem far-fetched to those who follow established religious traditions, it will soon become normal and touted as giving

---

[92] "Deus ex machina: former Google engineer is developing an AI god," September 28, 2017, https://www.theguardian.com/technology/2017/sep/28/artificial-intelligence-god-anthony-levandowski

[93] "An AI god will emerge by 2042 and write its own bible. Will you worship it?" October 2, 2017, https://venturebeat.com/ai/an-ai-god-will-emerge-by-2042-and-write-its-own-bible-will-you-worship-it/

[94] "Deus ex machina: former Google engineer is developing an AI god," September 28, 2017, https://www.theguardian.com/technology/2017/sep/28/artificial-intelligence-god-anthony-levandowski

people additional choices to express spirituality in the modern day. We may think that we would never fall for such ideology, or that our children are immune to this, but keep in mind the ability of advanced AI to test, iterate, and improve persuasive messaging billions of times, in addition to the ability to give or withhold resources. The potential threat of this kind of automated preaching becomes huge.

What is the end result when our children have lost real heart-to-heart connections in their life, live in a world of increasingly fake digital relationships, disconnect from nature and the real world Allah created, and immerse themselves in virtual worlds? Rather than their heart being attached to Allah, many young people now grow up apathetic to the idea of religion and God. They grow up thinking that the only thing that provides anything for them is the digital world. Why care about the world around them when so many young people have no connection whatsoever with these elements of Allah's creation. *"What has God done for me? Why do I need Him. My smartphone, my AI friend, my digital world provide everything for me."* The dangers of digital *shirk* (associating partners with Allah) are greater than we may realise.

Pick Your Pandora's Box

If the Islamic approach to making decisions (both big and small) is a sophisticated balancing of potential harms and benefits, then AI will need to be examined with the same level of rational scrutiny and rigour: "A.I. indeed has the potential to help us defeat cancer, discover lifesaving drugs, and invent solutions for our climate and energy crises. There are innumerable other benefits we cannot begin to imagine. But it doesn't matter how high the skyscraper of benefits A.I. assembles if the foundation collapses."[95]

---

[95] "You Can Have the Blue Pill or the Red Pill, and We're Out of Blue Pills," March 24, 2023, https://www.nytimes.com/2023/03/24/opinion/yuval-harari-ai-chatgpt.html

This brings to mind the novels of George Orwell's *1984* and Aldous Huxley's *Brave New World*. In the former, an oppressive government uses pervasive surveillance to control the population, while in the latter, the fictional population is controlled through their addictions, uncontrolled pleasures, and desires. The Prophet ﷺ warned us of a time where mass deception, indulgence in desires, and outright denial of God will be widespread. What type of society are we racing to – an Orwellian one or a Huxleyan one?

Upgrading Humanity – Hurtling towards Transhumanism

As the size and cost of computer chips decreases and computational power and efficiency increases, we will move towards another milestone in which the very idea of making use of technology through navigating screens will seem old fashioned. The mere act of searching, reading, and curating information in a serial manner limits the amount of information a human can take on board.

AI has already surpassed human expert ability in many distinct and narrow domains. Once we have superhuman artificial intelligence, we can directly enhance the human body through a variety of implants to harness and rise above human limitations. We can become transhuman.

> **The Prophet ﷺ warned us of a time where mass deception, indulgence in desires, and outright denial of God will be widespread.**

Transhumanism is a philosophy that proposes that this kind of human augmentation improves the human condition. And they would be right, to some extent. We already use this technology in the form of pacemakers (heart augmentation), glasses (vision augmentation), or the devices in our pockets and on our wrists (mind augmentation) and there is no doubt that these have helped improve the quality of life for many people. For proponents of this philosophy, implants are merely a logical extension of the road we are already on that will continue to "improve" human abilities. All the information in the world will be available not just at our fingertips, but also in our brains. While the software for this reality is already on its way, the hardware, called a brain-computer interface (BCI) is still in its infancy.

BCIs have already been implanted in several clinical cases to restore normal body functionality after suffering from a debilitating injury. Examples include restoring the ability to control a prosthetic limb, allowing communication enhancement, and even vision restoration.[96]

When we add to this our growing knowledge in the fields of nanotechnology and synthetic biology, we will look and view all past versions of humanity as outdated, obsolete, and primitive.[97] Humanity has the potential, according to those in favour of this technology, to exponentially improve and transcend all past human limitations of intelligence, physical illness, and even the ultimate human limitation of death.

Reaching for The Tree of Immortality

If we consider technological progress as the journey to solving previously unsolvable problems, then for some, the pinnacle of human

---

[96] Kenney-Lang, E. et al, "Advancing Brain-Computer Interface Applications for Severely Disabled Children Through a Multidisciplinary National Network: Summary of the Inaugural Pediatric BCI Canada Meeting, Frontiers in Human Neuroscience, 2020, 14

[97] "AI and Transhumanism: Could Quest for Super-intelligence and Eternal Life Lead to a Dystopian Nightmare?," August, 1, 2017, https://www.newsweek.com/ai-transhumanism-super-intelligence-dystopian-nightmare-644128

achievement seems to point to immortality – the ultimate unsolvable problem. We are already seduced to buy products that promise youth. We will soon be promised life extensions and many more years of high quality living with the eventual promise of "living as long as we want to".

Of course, this promise is not new. Our father and mother, Adam and Eve were expelled from the heavenly garden by the devil's temptation for the same thing. The Qur'an unequivocally promises that every soul shall taste death (Qur'an 3:185; 29:57). While Muslims should seek to have a high-quality long life in obedience to Allah and righteous works, true immortality is a fruitless goal. The Prophet ﷺ reminds us that "the world is the prison for the believer, and a paradise for the disbeliever" (Muslim). Our true everlasting life, is that of the Hereafter.

Philosophical Foundations

What world view is guiding and fuelling technological progress in this direction? When we look at the question of what and how, the answers seem reasonable and understandable. However, when we start to ask why, the answers make more sense from a materialist-atheist point of view.

If humanity is truly a meaningless accident of a random, purely material universe that came from nothingness and is going to end in nothingness, then the urgency of this technological game makes more sense. If the only purpose is to sustain a hedonistic, pleasure-filled way of life and to attempt to become immortal and simulate a heaven on earth through technological augmentation, then the picture becomes clearer and more complete. It then also makes sense that AI should play a significant role in accelerating humanity towards the virtual world and further away from the real world with all its challenges.

The Qur'an is constantly reminding us to connect with Allah by connecting with His signs through the natural world. We are challenged

> **" What world view is guiding and fuelling technological progress in this direction? "**

to reflect on the universe and its vastness, the earth in its alternations, the sun in its arc, the moon in its stages, and countless other dependent realities that foster wonder, humility, and gratitude towards the sole, independent, necessary, Divine source.

However, when we spend most of our time disconnected from these realities and connected to a "competing" virtual world replete with empty entertainment, artificial friends, mostly irrelevant information, and over-hyped news cycles within climate-controlled rooms, then it is easier to grow up feeling like the virtual world is the provider of all our needs. All the food, entertainment, friends, and comforts we can ever want are not even a click away, they are a thought away. Through augmentation, we can even attempt to escape the ultimate inescapable destination of death. What need do we have to ponder purpose, develop character, or even strengthen our mind and body?

Ironically, like other examples of modern-day abundance that actually induce suffering, living in an AI-enabled digital bubble will only exacerbate mental illnesses and *dis*-ease.

Artificial intelligence-fuelled technological advances will be ubiquitous, subtle, and somewhat unavoidable. However, just like the other technologies we have discussed, it is worth us being educated about their benefits and harms, keeping our inner-eye open and proceeding with caution.

TIME TO MAKE **BETTER CHOICES**

5

Personal Principles of Change

"I agree with you, but what can I do, there is no other way in this day and age..."

The challenge of living in these times while avoiding the harms mentioned so far may seem daunting and perhaps even impossible. In this chapter, we will explore practical and achievable steps for any sincere seeker of change to move in the right direction.

Since applications and technology will continuously develop and change, a good starting point is to consider the principles by which we can make decisions now and in the future, regardless of the circumstances or the magnitude of the decision.

Decision Making Principles

The following is a list of general principles to keep in mind, which have been drawn from our rich Islamic legal and spiritual legacy. These principles are very useful not only for making digital choices, but decision making for life in general.

1. **Weigh the benefits and harms of each possible decision and choose the decision with most net benefit.** Identify the benefits and harms of each alternative decision and then list them. Assign a number to each from 1 to 10. Add up the scores in the benefits column and subtract the scores in the harm column. The decision with the greatest value is the one to make.

   Remember to consider both spiritual and worldly benefits and harms. If it helps, you can share this with a trusted and learned person, who can help you see any factors you may not have thought of.

2. **Preventing harm takes precedence over gaining benefit.** If after applying the first principle, there is a similar level of both harm and benefit, then it is better to forgo the benefits of the decision in order to prevent harm.

3. **Block means that will lead to probable harm.** If a benefit will open the door to probable (not just theoretical) equal or greater harm, then it is better to forgo the benefits.

4. **Base decisions on the most probable or average outcomes and not exceptions or rarities.** Think honestly about what would be

the probable outcome of the decision and prioritise that above exceptions and unlikely outcomes in any decision making.

5. **Stay clear of the boundaries.** The *nafs*, when left unregulated, will transgress. Choose limits that stay well within the bounds of what is permissible in Islamic law. If we continue to walk on the edge of permissibility, there is every chance that we will eventually cross over into the harmful and ultimately impermissible. What Allah has made impermissible for us is for our own protection and well-being.

6. **Do not give preference to conveniences over needs and necessities.** As we saw in Chapter One benefits can be conveniences, necessities or needs. It is not worth pursuing a convenience if it results in us losing a need, and it is not worth pursuing a need over a necessity when it comes to matters of religion, well-being, family, property or reputation. This means making tough choices and letting go of lesser and perhaps more immediate benefits for greater ones that may not be so apparent to us right now, no matter what the marketing ads are convincing us to do.

7. **Consider the effect of decisions, not only on yourself, but of the subsequent effects on those connected to you.** This includes family, friends, students, co-workers, and humanity at large. It may be that a decision that is personally beneficial for us may negatively impact those around us, so the net effect is one of harm.

8. **The value of anything is based on how it will "play out" on the Day of Judgement.** Some things will be very beneficial for us on that Day while others will be very harmful. What is worthless on that Day is essentially harmful as it is lost energy and time in what could have been used for good. It should be an essential element in decision making to take this long term perspective and define what we mean by ultimate success.

9 **We alone will not be able to make the best decision.** At every stage of decision making, ask for guidance from Allah through *istikhāra* (prayer of seeking good). Internalise and actualise that we have no ability to decide anything on our own. We must rely completely on Allah.

Coming back more specifically to digital decisions and based on the above principles, we can conclude that under the vast majority of circumstances:

- **Less is Better.** The less we use digital devices and apps, the better, even if this means giving up some of the benefits.
- **Removing Accessibility is Best.** Sometimes it is just easier not to have access to that device or that app, instead of struggling to reduce its usage.

So how can we implement this?

Setting Intentions

We have seen that the more digitally connected we are, the more:
- Addicted we will become
- Our base *nafs* is strengthened and its vulnerabilities capitalised on
- We sacrifice privacy and choice, and
- We are contributing to an unethical system of surveillance and manipulation of others.
- We will be negatively impacted by the numerous and diverse harms discussed in the previous chapters.

Therefore, a good starting point would be to make a specific written or verbal intention to reduce our digital engagement in order to be free of this addiction, to strengthen our control over our *nafs*, to prioritise our privacy and choice, and to not be a party to an unethical system, and to save ourselves overall from the numerous harms discussed.

Next, we need to have a clear vision in our mind of what our targeted future relationship with the digital world looks like. This should be something that is practically achievable given our personal situations.

Then, we need to set small interim steps to achieve that target within some defined time frame. Our responsibility is to act on those steps at some level every day, no matter how minimal it is. Some days will be better than others, but the important thing is that we keep moving in the right direction and not compare ourselves with others, unless this will motivate us further. Our specific circumstances will shape our individual path.

We cannot give up because the journey is not perfect or the path is a little difficult. Just because we did not or could not take all the steps we would have liked to take, just because we are not where we would like to be, just because we had a bad day, it does not mean that we should not take any steps at all.

Once we commit to a step or a few steps, we do our best to stick to them. There will be exceptions. However, we have to deal with exceptions when they arise and see them as temporary blips in the path, not as an excuse to live our life constantly in "exception-mode".

"Islamicising" our current digital habits and choices is not the solution. We need to return to a baseline of mentally and emotionally uprooting all digital programs and devices from the equation, and only then analyse what to accept or reject based on the decision making principles explained above.

Forming Good Digital Habits

These specific habits will help along the journey to change in a positive manner when it comes to our relationship with the digital world.

Digital Habit #1: The need for friction
A very simple practical tool to decrease device usage is to purposely place friction between us and our device or app. Once we have identified what we need to reduce, we simply need to make it harder to access. In other words, we create an extra hurdle to serve as a deterrent for the *nafs* from indulging in the harmful or unnecessary. For example:

- Putting the laptop in a drawer as opposed to leaving it open on a desk
- Turning off the wireless router as a default and only turning it on when needed
- Keeping the smartphone in a different room so that we have to get up to access it
- Using programs on the computer or phone that block access from certain apps at certain times of the day or week and require extra steps to override them.

As trivial as these steps sounds, they are a great starting point to help wean off our digital dependence.

Digital Habit #2: Digital fasting
The purpose of fasting – of refraining from food and drink – is *taqwa* or Allah-consciousness (Qur'an 2:183). By learning to refuse our *nafs* in the basic needs of food and drink, we gain strength over our desires and freedom to be more aware of the Divine. The same principle applies when we refrain from digital means that are actively distracting us from Allah.

Digital fasting or detox can be as simple as having a screen-free block of time each day, a designated screen-free day once a week or even a hard two week screen-free retreat. We can begin detox in a way that works for us while pushing the *nafs* slightly outside the comfort zone and build on from there.

Many people find that, after an initial uncomfortable period, they feel liberated and have so much more time to engage in meaningful pursuits that they thought they didn't have time for.

Digital Habit #3: Batching

Imagine walking outside your house to check your mailbox every hour. Imagine going to the supermarket several times a day to buy something or check a price. Imagine going to the bank every day to make deposits or withdrawals.

It is pretty clear from these examples that this is not the best way to manage time or complete tasks; it would be so much more efficient to batch. Batching tasks means to set aside a certain time in the day or week to fulfil a task efficiently and with full focus and attention. This means designating set times of the day, week or month for tackling specific tasks. We already do this for jobs such as shopping, paperwork and cleaning.

However, strangely when it comes to our digital tasks, we are impulsive, haphazard and inefficient. We check our email and messages multiple times in an hour, our online bank account daily, and "visit" online markets at the whim of our desires. Because of the ease of access to these functions at the touch of a screen, we have unknowingly become dysfunctional impulsive people. Not only is it highly inefficient, but each time we act on an impulse we only strengthen the addictive pathways in the brain and so keep ourselves in the loop of continuing these bad habits.

A simple concept that can help us is to imagine our digital tasks as physical places. If we had to actually drive all the way to the supermarket or the bank, how would we schedule it? Similarly, for our digital tasks, we need to set aside specific days or times to "visit" those virtual places. We can set aside a day of the week for digital purchases, and throughout the week keep a list of things that come to mind that we need to buy. Similarly with online banking, we can batch all our transactions, and only check emails at specific times of the day.

Once we get into the habit of batching, we will find that we can be more organised, more focused on the task at hand and more efficient.

Digital Habit #4: Say 'no' to multitasking

If you were to visit the supermarket several times a day, you would consider it a waste of time to drive back and forth. In the same way, we waste time mentally jumping back and forth between mental tasks. Each time we interrupt a task to check Amazon or Gmail, it takes the brain at least 30 minutes to focus back again on the original task.[98]

The antidote to this time wasting is for us to simply not multitask. Say 'no' to checking messages while taking an online class. Say 'no' to scrolling through the news while sitting at the dinner table. Say 'no' to responding to that notification while talking to someone.

This will help us to be more mindful and engaged in the tasks that we are doing and enjoy them more fully.

Digital Habit #5: Unbundling

Our digital devices have been designed to bundle as many services and conveniences as possible into one sleek gadget, to increase our reliance and attachment to them. So when we are without our smartphone, it feels like we have lost a limb. We have seen in Chapter One that the implication of this is that we lose focus in our daily lives, in our relationships, in our worship.

---

98 "This Is Nuts: It Takes Nearly 30 Minutes to Refocus After You Get Distracted," June 19, 2020, https://www.themuse.com/advice/this-is-nuts-it-takes-nearly-30-minutes-to-refocus-after-you-get-distracted

The way to claim back this focus is to adopt the habit of unbundling – that is going back to having specific, limited devices in our lives that perform their function when needed. That means having a phone that is only a phone, a camera that is only a camera, an audio player that is only an audio player and ensuring that none of these devices is connected to the internet. The only device that would be connected to the internet is the computer and we will have a look at what precautions can be taken in that regard later in this chapter.

The table below serves as a guide to unbundling the tasks on a smartphone.

Smartphone function	Unbundling alternative
Phonecalls	Home or simple phone
Telling time	Wrist or pocket watch
Alarm	Alarm clock
Salāh times	Print out of monthly salāh times/salāh watches
Qiblah (salāh direction)	Compass/salāh watches
Listening to audio	MP3 player
Taking pictures	Camera
Travel directions	Print directions/GPS device
Messaging	Desktop applications (e.g. Telegram)
Email and internet usage	Desktop/laptop computer

Is it easier and more cost effective to have all of these features in one small device? Quite frankly, yes.

Is it *better*? That is where we must pause and remember all the issues and principles introduced in the previous chapters. We cannot continue to compromise the quality of our lives based on the argument that it is cheaper and more convenient. Think about other areas of our life where we would not put convenience over quality.

Adopting Healthy Online Practices

These are some general online practices that it would be good for us to adopt and to encourage in our families as well:

1. Avoid using platforms that are made by companies who profit off our data. We will be making specific recommendations later in this chapter.

2. Try to use devices offline as much as possible.

3. Implement digital privacy practices. We would not declare our personal information (address, credit card information, contact details) in public, and the same boundaries apply in the virtual arena. We can make a habit of accessing the internet through a Virtual Private Network or VPN, which allows us to access the internet with a certain level of privacy. There are various VPN programs we can download for our computer or smartphone, with an array of paid and free options to choose from.

4. Become familiar with the concept of encryption, which is the process where readable text is scrambled/coded, only to be unscrambled by the intended recipient. This adds another layer of data security. We can choose communication platforms that have end-to-end encryption.

5. Choose safe, secure browsers to access the internet.

6. Utilise a password manager for all our online accounts. It is so tempting to create one easy to remember password for all of our accounts or save all our passwords in a document on the computer,

but these are not safe practices and leave us vulnerable to having our accounts hacked. Complex, generated passwords using password managers are the safest option.

7   Avoid the use of social media as much as possible, and we should certainly avoid posting pictures of ourselves, our family and friends.

Specific Recommendations

Here we offer specific recommendations regarding devices and apps with a layered approach that can be tailored according to your personal situation and stage in your digital resetting journey.

Level 1 recommendations are basic level steps that everyone can take to begin their digital detox journey. For those who may already be implementing these recommendations, they can advance to the Level 2 recommendations. At the most advanced level are the Level 3 recommendations.

Our success is through gradual, consistent change, not sudden impulsive overhauls that fizzle out after a few days. We take a few small practical steps at a time consistently and regularly, we plan for the challenges and sacrifices that may come ahead, and we seek the assistance of Allah throughout. As the Prophet ﷺ said, "The most beloved acts by Allah are those that are consistent, even if they are few" (Bukhari).

Smartphones

When we talk about the harms of the digital world (on our health and well-being, relationships, worship, privacy and surveillance), the vast majority of these come down to the ownership of a smartphone. It follows, therefore, that the most effective solution to mitigating the harms is, happily, to not own one. *This may be the best decision we ever make.*

We realise that that may not be possible at this stage, but there are a great many steps we can take to limit our access to a smartphone and thus our dependence. The argument that we can own a smartphone and not be addicted to it, is one we have shown is not practically possible for most people given the addictive nature of the device itself. Below is a summary of our recommendations regarding smartphone use.

Level 1:
- Delete all apps that are sinful or lead to sinful behaviour.
- Delete all unnecessary apps.
- Do not use a smartphone for games or idle entertainment.
- Activate time limits on all other apps you feel you may be addicted to.
- Use an image blocker to avoid viewing impermissible unintended imagery.
- Do not sleep with your smartphone in your bedroom.
- Make it a rule not to check your smartphone first thing in the morning nor make it the last thing you look at before you go to sleep.
- Turn off as many sound or visual app notifications as possible.
- Do not carry your smartphone with you into the masjid or a class of knowledge, unless absolutely necessary, in which case make sure it is completely silenced.
- Detox from your smartphone every once in a while for a period of time. Give it to someone else, put it out of sight or leave it at home when you go out. This time away from your device will help you see what you actually miss and what you do out of habit. This will help you make better decisions going forward.
- Do not provide a smartphone for someone under the age of 18.

Level 2:
- Have daily detox periods from your smartphone.
- Use your smartphone for **specific required** tasks only, or at specific set times. Even then, only use it for what you need it for.
- Try having to sign in with a username and password to your apps every time you wish to use them instead of always having instant

access to them. This creates an extra layer of friction and will reduce unnecessary usage.
- Move as many apps as you can from your smartphone to a laptop or desktop computer.
- If you have data on your smartphone, turn it on only at set times or for specific non-frequent purposes.
- Convert your smartphone into a "dumb phone" by limiting as many internet based apps as possible.

Level 3:
- Do not **own** a smartphone.
- Use the unbundling table to replace the functions of your smartphone.
- Use a home phone/landline/"dumb phone" to make local calls.
- Use a landline with an international plan or a computer/tablet based app for international calls. Signal and Telegram both allow users to call one another from a computer and are more secure apps (Signal is the more secure).
- Consider scheduling in more face-to-face meetings.

Instant Messaging

This is probably one of the hardest aspects of a smartphone to let go of. Instant messaging allows us to communicate quickly, easily and without having to actually speak to someone. We can know looking at the ticks in the corner of the message, whether our message has been delivered and when that person has read it, all without any further effort on our part. Now we believe that we cannot live without instant messaging but is that really true? The first layer of recommendations looks at changing this mindset.

Level 0:
- Ask yourself: What are the pitfalls of instant messaging? Do I want to get caught up in the addictive back and forth of exchanges with all the misunderstandings that that can cause? Do I have to

rely on messaging as my prime means of communication? Is it a necessity or a need?
- Thinking back over the last week, what other options did I have for communication? Could I have met that person, called them, used a video meeting, emailed them?
- Am I hiding behind the façade of instant messaging because I would rather avoid real human contact? What does that tell me about my relationships and my interpersonal skills?
- Do I really need my communications to be instant and the responses to be immediate? Is it really an emergency or am I acting out of a false sense of urgency that is fuelled by my use of the device? And if I do need an urgent response, wouldn't it better to call that person?
- What would my life look like without instant messaging? Am I open to the possibility that my communications might be more meaningful, more organised, less overwhelming, better quality, more private and more secure? As opposed to a large, inefficient, distracting, and low quality mess where there are no boundaries between my personal and work life?

Once we have set in our mind the harms of messaging, it will be easier to implement the changes. Without this step, it becomes more of a struggle to phase away from this addictive function of our smartphones.

Level 1:
- Keep messaging on both a smartphone and a computer. However, only use secure platforms that allow usage from a computer without a smartphone. This allows you to have an extended time away from your smartphone in a bid to reduce your time with it.
- Batch your messaging. Have set times of the day or week and set purposes for messaging as opposed to open ended messaging at any time of day or night. Disable the messaging app outside of this set time.

- Use non-secure messaging platforms to the extent that is absolutely necessary. For example, if you have to communicate with someone and cannot use any other means.
- Remove yourself from any unnecessary chat groups or channels
- Let contacts know to call and visit more, and when needed, email as opposed to text/message.
- Apply the principles of Islamic etiquette to your messaging. If you would not say it to someone's face, then do not put it in a message. If it would be haram in a face-to-face setting, then it is likely haram in a message context. When possible, carbon copy a third person when communicating with someone of the opposite gender.

Level 2:
- Keep chatting/messaging, but only through secure applications and only through a computer and not a smartphone.
- Replace family and friends and community group chats with group video and phone calls and in person meetings, where geography allows. We need to normalise meeting regularly and more often with one another. There is more *barakah* (blessing) in being physically present together and, if not, then through at least our voices. These interactions are more personal and meaningful than an avalanche of messages in groups where we don't know half of the participants or misunderstand the meaning intended by the sender.
- Similarly meet with work colleagues either in person or via video and phone calls to discuss actual matters that need attention. These meetings are more likely to be productive as they have a discrete beginning and end and everyone is focused to the matter at hand. You can meet as often as you need to accommodate the needs of the group and issues not addressed can usually simply wait until the next meeting. If you need to call for an urgent, previously unplanned meeting, you can do that as well.
- For both work and personal groups, group emails can be used for electronic information transfer through secure emailing

alternatives such as Groups.io. Organisations and groups can take advantage of the concept of email digests, which accumulates multiple emails into one email over the day or week.
- Use mass texting software to send messages to everyone's simple phone for time-sensitive announcements to a group of people.
- For an event that needs real time communication with members, such as an overseas trip, a chat group can be set up on a secure platform for that specific event, and then deactivated afterwards.

Level 3:
- Uproot the concept of instant chatting/messaging from your life. Remove all instant chatting/messaging platforms and discontinue this means of communication.
- Use a simple text messages when truly a phone call or meeting won't do.

Beyond Messages
Because instant messaging is such an insidious part of our lives, we would like to come back to this issue of mindset. We need to remind ourselves that our interactions with friends, family, co-workers and even strangers should be centred around conscious, attentive, quality communication. We need to take the time to develop bonds that are stronger, more authentic, and more likely to lead to positive learning experiences from everyone we communicate with. We do not need to have hundreds of contacts and connections that do not contribute to our personal and communal development and growth.

We need to cultivate a mindset in which it is welcomed to initiate real contact, to visit someone, to call someone. This does not disturb them or offend them. This is what real relationships and community is based on. This is what humanity is. It is making real contact and facing real emotions and encountering situations. Simply hiding behind a message should be, in many cases at least, viewed as impolite and impersonal.

So when there is an event in our community, our family, our social circle, when there is a birth, a death, an illness, we need to visit or at least call as a minimum. It should not be acceptable to simply send a message itself, while calling or visiting was feasible. Similarly, we should refrain from the practice of sending out mass, cutely designed messages and videos at Eid and bring back the beautiful Prophetic habit of visiting each other, and when we cannot, then at least call.

Social Media

Social media has been advertised and marketed as an innocent means to simply connect people and we have seen that it is, in reality, addictive by design, socially and morally corrupting for most of us, and a platform for a plethora of sin of almost all types.

For those who would like to read more on the harms of social media, they can refer to Jaron Lanier's book *Ten Arguments for Deleting Your Social Media Accounts Right Now*. Meanwhile, these are the recommendations we would suggest:

Level 1:
- Turn off social media notifications.
- Limit the platforms that you are on and the number of accounts that you have.
- Delete unsecure platforms such as Facebook, Instagram and Twitter from your smartphone.
- Check your accounts only at set times and reduce those times gradually as much as possible.
- Make a commitment to stop using social media for what is unnecessary – posting pictures, commenting unnecessarily, browsing and scrolling for no set purpose.
- Do not make non-professional connections with the opposite gender.
- Make sure your image blocker is on when using social media to prevent impermissible or harmful imagery from making its way to your eyes and heart.

- Do not allow children still under your supervision to have any social media accounts. No child needs a social media account and it is nearly impossible for them to use it responsibly if they do.

Level 2:
- Use specific social media platforms for a specific purpose, such as business, recruitment or organisational marketing.
- Do not use social media for idle entertainment or for simply "connecting" with family and friends, while there are better means to truly connect.
- Take extended periods of time out from social media to gain a perspective on how much you actually need it and whether your quality of life would benefit from removing it altogether.

Level 3:
- Delete all social media accounts for good. Once you have spent extended periods of time away from social media, it is often liberating and increases quality of life for yourself and those around you. You find, most likely, that this is something that you simply do not need in your life.

Internet

It is without doubt that the internet has an abundance of benefits. It also harbours a black hole of sins that any one of us and our children can access with a click. With this understanding, we need to engage with the internet only when truly needed with an awareness of Allah, get what we need, and then exit.

Our Prophet ﷺ teaches us, "The most despised places in the sight of Allah are the markets" (Muslim). If this is applicable to a fruit or a clothing market, what about the digital market, whose commodities themselves are corrupting?

The word *sūq* in Arabic means market and is derived from the root verb *sāqa,* which means to drive or herd. No wonder marketers use the term "herding" to essentially refer to manipulating others for their selfish purposes. Interestingly, the word "herding" reminds us of the base *bahīmī naf*s (cattle-like self) marketers operate on, for *bahā'im* (cattle) are the ones meant to be herded, not people.

These are recommendations to limit the impact of the internet in the home:

Level 1:
- Continue having unlimited internet access at home but turn it on only at set times or for specific functions. This means that everyone in the household obtains what they need from the internet within a specified block of time and then it is turned off.
- Turn the router off at bed time.
- Consider only accessing the internet through a wired connection, as opposed to a wireless router. This will help limit its accessibility in the home to specific locations, and it is also safer from a health perspective as it reduces electromagnetic radiation, which is another major concern with our technological devices.
- Access the internet through a Virtual Private Network (VPN), which allows you to access the internet anonymously because of ethical concerns around the concept of stating you are at a location that you are really not.
- Ensure that the important information on your computer is encrypted. Use encrypted emails (such as Protonmail), and choose stronger passwords or use a password manager.
- Block certain websites or apps that you know you are not able to control and only lead to hours of mindless time wasting or sin.
- Activate computer settings to also put time limits on apps and internet use.
- Use a secure browser with ad, tracking, and image blocking plug-ins.

- Keep any computers in an open common area in the house. Avoid allowing children to use their laptops privately.

Level 2:
- Have limited internet access inside the house, in addition to using the internet outside the house when needed. Turn the internet inside the house off and based on need.

Level 3:
- Use it only outside the home as needed through a VPN (i.e. at a public library, for example).

Online Learning

Education for all ages has recently seen a significant shift from being face-to-face to taking place online thanks to the Covid pandemic in 2019. With the many benefits this brings, a lot of harm has also been introduced. Learning quality for most students has taken a significant hit as many students attend class while fiddling with two or three other apps on the computer. It has become the norm to search for answers online and to copy and paste these for homework. We must also understand that sitting passively in front of a screen is not the most interactive means of education for our students and so it is little wonder that many of them gain little educational value from being online.

The convenience of studying Islam online comes at the price of the loss of the many spiritual benefits that come from learning at the feet of Islamic scholars and being in physical circles of knowledge. A core component of such physical circles is not just the knowledge itself, but also the companionship of those that one is learning from and with. Historically, sacred knowledge was believed to be passed on through the medium of the heart as well as through that of the intellect. Through observing our teachers we learn so much more, and being in their company is a blessing in which there is much good. Thus, learning online should remain as one scholar put it, the *"tayammum"* (dry ablution) of learning, only "valid" when water (face-to-face learning) is unavailable.

Below is a summary of our recommendations regarding online learning:

- Resort to online learning only when face-to-face options are not available, would impose significant hardship, or would result in being in a physical environment that is not healthy for your soul or body.
- When you are in an online class, close or disable all other applications on your device. Use program blockers to help control the *nafs* from distractions and digital wandering.
- Act as if you were in a physical class. For example, and especially when seeking sacred knowledge: dress as if you were in class, do not eat or drink, do not have a phone or other device on or near you, turn your phone off, sit yourself attentively. Come to class early, eager to learn and prepared to focus, and sit down slowly not in rushed manner.
- Keep your learning/study area free from clutter, tidy and organised as this will help your learning.
- Use the computer only as a window/portal into the class. For example, if you are using an iPad for learning, you can lock the screen once the class window is open so that you cannot be tempted to fiddle with the device during the class.
- Sit at a distance from the computer.
- Take online classes that recommend the use of a hardcopy book and notebook while in class as opposed to being completely virtual-reliant.
- Learning online should not be unstructured. It is too easy for students to say they have schoolwork and then to end up being online all day. Just as a physical class would have a beginning and end time, so should an online one. Studies not completed within the allocated window of time can wait until the next window. This allows time to take a break outside and increases the efficacy of what has been learnt.

- When possible choose online audio over video to prevent the harm of digital imagery.
- Take classes in a communal area of the home. The presence of other family members acts as a deterrent from using the computer in spiritually and intellectually harmful ways.

Video games

The harms of video games have already been expanded on in Chapter Two. The simple answer to the issue of video games is to eliminate them completely from our lives. Their destructive harms, including their very strong addictive pull of the young and not-so-young, almost always far outweigh any benefits.

As an adult, we would make no other recommendation than to **stop all use of all video games immediately.** This may well require a period of support, counselling or even therapy and we would encourage that these are sought as needed.

As parents, one of the most positive acts we can do is to not introduce our children to video games in the first place. It is so easy to give in to our peer pressure, their peer pressure, the narrative that it is harmless fun, our child's tears and demands. We can remember that it is easier to say a compassionate but firm 'no' with an explanation, and offer an alternative than accompany our children to an addiction clinic. There is no such thing as moderate use of video games. There is no such thing as remaining in control.

If we have children that engage with video games, we need to wean them off sooner rather than later and we will discuss in Chapter Six what support we can offer our children through this.

Which Platforms and Apps Should I be Using?

Within the recommendations that we have made above, we often suggest switching apps or browsers. In this section, we make specific recommendations of which platforms and apps are more secure and which ones are not.

While the underlying technology and privacy policies are constantly being updated, there are four important considerations in choosing a private and secure messaging app: end-to-end encryption, transparency of the underlying code, the storage/sharing of user data (and metadata), and the company's business model.

With regards to end-to-end encryption, Signal is the best. WhatsApp has implemented the same underlying encryption protocol (i.e. Open Whisper Systems) as Signal, which is the gold standard. Telegram has a separate end-to-end encryption protocol, but unlike Signal, it is not default for all messages.

Transparency is also an important consideration with regards to having an active community of third party researchers that can audit open source code to ensure it is not being used in nefarious ways. Of the three messaging apps, WhatsApp has the least open source code, while Signal is completely open sourced. Telegram is in the middle with a closed back-end, but has open source for other parts of its system.

In terms of data and metadata storage, Signal collects the least and WhatsApp collects the most. Even though the data is encrypted, this still matters because metadata can be used to make some surprisingly accurate conclusions about the user's life. In 2016, Signal received a subpoena requiring them to provide information about two Signal users to a federal grand jury. According to Signal, the only information they had in their possession to share was "the date and time a user registered with Signal and the last date of a user's connectivity to the Signal service."[99]

Finally, it is important to take into account how the company makes money. WhatsApp had originally billed itself as an end-to-end encrypted solution with no access to user data. However, Facebook eagerly purchased WhatsApp for $19 billion in 2014. We have previously discussed the reality of Facebook's privacy practices and business model. Knowing that Facebook monetises user data through targeted advertising of products and ideas, it makes sense why they would want access to obtain the data of more than 2 billion users. *If past behaviour is any indicator of future behaviour, Facebook's long history of questionable privacy practices should be a red flag to anyone who understands the seriousness of lack of privacy.*

Taking all these considerations into account, as of the time of writing, Signal has the most robust combination of privacy and security features, with Telegram coming in second.[100,101] While WhatsApp has improved the underlying encryption protocol it uses, its lack of transparency, its manner of storing/sharing user data, and its underlying business model make it problematic for users seeking privacy and security.

Finally, on a more subtle note, every time we choose to use a messaging or social media platform, even for very good reasons, we are contributing to the validation of its usage. When we message someone back and forth on WhatsApp, Facebook, or Instagram, with perhaps important Islamic knowledge and advice, we are at the same time further validating reliance on that platform.

---

99 "Grand jury subpoena for Signal user data, Eastern District of Virginia," October 4, 2016, https://signal.org/bigbrother/eastern-virginia-grand-jury/

100 "Secure Messaging App Showdown: WhatsApp vs. Signal," April 30, 2017, https://lifehacker.com/secure-messaging-app-showdown-whatsapp-vs-signal-1794684943

101 "Why you should switch to Signal or Telegram from WhatsApp, Today ...," November 25, 2018, https://medium.com/@contactsunny/why-you-should-switch-to-signal-or-telegram-from-whatsapp-today-fa773694d05e

So, we *must avoid, to the best of our abilities, using platforms, apps, and programs from companies whose business model is to monetise and profit off users' behavioural data through the collection, sale, and exchange of that data to other entities.*

The two largest companies contributing to this are Google and Facebook and so we must first strive to avoid using any of their products.

Alternatives to Google

Google is so ubiquitous that it may seem impossible to avoid, but alternatives exist.[102] Below is a list of common Google applications and alternatives that you can consider using instead.

> *Google Search:* Instead, switch to search engines that keep you anonymous and do not track or gather your data. Alternatives include DuckDuckGo and Startpage.
>
> *Google Chrome:* Firefox is a great alternative. It is a nonprofit company whose business model does not revolve around gathering and selling your data. Firefox has many default plug-ins to protect you from website trackers and cookies, and many other valuable plug-ins, such as image blockers. Other options include Tor browser, Iridium, Brave, and Waterfox. A private and secure browser is an essential tool you need when travelling within the world wide web.
>
> *Gmail:* Safer and more secure options include Tutanota, Mailfence, Protonmail, and Posteo to name a few.
>
> *Google Groups:* Other alternatives exist such as groups.io for email groups.

---

102 "Alternatives to Google Products (Complete List for 2020)," June 24, 2019, https://restoreprivacy.com/google-alternatives/

Google Voice: This may appear to be free, but remember what price you are paying. There are alternative internet voice options.

Google Maps: An alternative is OpenStreetMap.

Google Drive: Nextcloud is an open-source platform that can be used instead. Dropbox is a commonly used alternative but is not the best in terms of privacy.

Google Docs: You can explore CryptPad, Mailfence Documents, and Zoho Docs.

YouTube: Invidio.us allows you to watch any YouTube video anonymously. If you need to access YouTube, make sure you are not signed in, and only watch what is necessary. As a general rule, our knowledge needs to come from books, audio, and directly from people and not from videos.

Google Hangouts: Signal and Telegram are good alternatives.

Alternatives to Facebook

Facebook and Instagram personal accounts: We would recommend deleting these

Facebook and Instagram business accounts: Some business and organisations may wish to retain a Facebook page for their company. We would recommend having this information elsewhere as well so that any of your customers can access your content in ways other than social media, for example, your own company platform.

WhatsApp: Signal or Telegram are more secure alternatives.

The Necessity of Alternatives

The wisdom of our beautiful religion teaches us that, **"Emptying must proceed beautifying."** Before we can fill the "cup" of our life with good, we need to remove the evil and even gradually the reprehensible and the useless. Only then will we have room to be able to fill it with what is more beautiful and meaningful for us in this world and the next. We have so far looked at the need for emptying and letting go of what is holding us down in our pursuit of higher aims and a better quality of life. However, emptying alone is insufficient.

If we do not fill the cup of our life with goodness, it will soon become refilled with what we had previously emptied it of. As Imam Shafi'i said, "The lower self, if you do not pre-occupy it with good, it will pre-occupy you with evil."

So in parallel with freeing ourselves and our families of digital addictions and distractions, we must also try to fill our lives with healthier and more nourishing activities. Life is so vast and deep, but we seem to have acquired short sightedness while staring at our screens and forgotten what a spiritually focused, purposeful, offline and screen-free life involves. Here are a few examples:

Nature · Calling family · Biking · PAINTING · Family time · Visiting others · Cooking · Storytelling · Nasheeds · Reflection · Travelling · Tea time · Martial arts · Arts · Fishing · Dhikr · Cycling · Sewing · Seeking knowledge · Woodwork · Gardening · Visiting the sick · Pottery · Mosque · Hosting guests · Hiking · Volunteering · Crafts · Dawah · Camping · Chores · Writing · Home projects

Choose the Way of Taqwa

An essential tool in developing a healthier relationship with the digital world is simply to learn to "choose the way of *taqwa* (Allah-consciousness)" through employing the principles and the tools outlined in this chapter as well as having an overall active awareness and prioritisation in life of what really matters. In the digital age, we have to take the path of *taqwa* with our digital devices.

1. This means first eliminating the impermissible for ourselves and our family. This includes impermissible images, impermissible music, and impermissible speech such as gossip and backbiting.
2. Next we can work towards eliminating disliked use, such as wasting time.
3. Then we can elevate to the way of *ihsān* (spiritual excellence), and limit our engagement with digital devices and platforms to only what is purposeful, in a manner that pleases Allah and His Messenger ﷺ. We need to learn to always prefer spiritual over worldly gain and thus eternal over temporary gain.
4. The final steps in this path are to practise a healthy level of *zuhd* (abstinence) in removing the unnecessary or wasteful from our lives and replacing it with what is more beneficial to us. This requires us to monitor the signals of our heart to detect what moves it in the right direction and what moves it in the wrong direction. Our heart is our most precious asset, our essence, and what we will return to Allah with on the Day of Judgement: "The Day on which neither wealth will be of any use, nor children, except the one who comes to Allah with a sound heart" (Qur'an 26:88-89). We need to choose those things that will increase the soundness of our heart.

6

Parenting in the Digital Age

Parenting has always been one of the most blessed yet difficult responsibilities humans take on. When we add the layer of digital considerations of raising children in the modern age, things get especially complex and confusing for a parent who is sincerely trying to do the best job they can.

Like any other endeavour, it first helps to define the desired outcome. Our job as parents is not simply to ensure the merely physical survival of the next generation. That is an ambition shared by and executed by the animal kingdom. As a vicegerent of Allah, everything we do is in pursuit of Divine pleasure and acceptance. Parenting, then, is the effort to please the Divine by doing our utmost best to raise children that the Divine will be pleased with.

A number of parents take a hands-off, wait and watch approach with regards to digital technologies in their children's lives. The commonly held belief is that parents cannot shield their children from everything, while knowing that there are pitfalls out there. These parents trust that their children are smart enough to work through whatever challenges will come their way.

What is interesting about this kind of parenting is that we wouldn't use this same line of reasoning for other areas, such as their education or career choices. Instead, we try to prepare our children's education to the best of our ability so that they do not have to face unnecessary challenges further down the line.

In addition, children can be quite adept at managing the perception of their parents, so by the time that any issues visibly surface to the parents' attention, the problems are quite advanced. Much damage will likely have already been done, and it will require much more energy to rectify. The damage look like addictions, academic challenges, inappropriate relationships, and mental health issues to name a few.

Some parents are more proactive in their parenting approach and take advice from parenting specialists. Unfortunately some parenting "specialists" today are recommending that parents get a social media account themselves to befriend their children online, so they can help monitor their children's use of social media. However well intentioned, these recommendations come about from not understanding what social media is really about and how it is designed.

As we have seen, social media is not a neutral platform, but is more like a casino, designed with an addictive purpose. No specialist would ever recommend to a parent to enter a casino and gamble along with their children to help monitor their children's gambling addiction. And what is to prevent children creating multiple ghost accounts in order to hide their activities from their parents?

A child's relationship with technology will be shaped, if not by their parents, then by peers from families with a different value system to ours, corporations with a financial incentive to monetise attention, or strangers with their own agendas.

While we cannot list detailed recommendations for parenting in regards to every digital technology that exists and will exist, we can offer seven principles for parents to consider as they build a healthy digital plan for their family.

Digital Parenting Principle #1: Show, Don't Tell

The best thing a parent can give their child is a real-life example of what a healthy relationship with digital tools looks like. Our actions will drown out all our words of caution if we are constantly looking down at our gadgets, while our children are tugging for our attention and longing for eye contact. Change must begin with us. The most important question parents must ask themselves is: Am I on the journey to a healthier relationship with digital technologies? We are not going for perfection, because that does not exist, especially in this arena. But we need to have an honest self awareness of our own challenges and be acting in some way on our path of improvement.

Digital Parenting Principle #2: Be Aware of Digital Needs versus Wants

Most of us cannot completely remove digital technologies from our or our children's lives. So, we must live with these highly addictive, privacy-invading, distraction-provoking devices around us. In some ways, the world today is setup in such a way that we must play with fire.

Having said that then it is most helpful for us to learn to differentiate and prioritise our necessities, needs, and conveniences. While we or our children begin by attending to a need, we very quickly get sucked into an ocean of wants that are all just a scroll, swipe and click away, the result being hours pass and we have not accomplished the task we set out to do in the first place. Every time we set out to do a task, we find other digital things vying for our attention and we have to overcome a mental hurdle to keep us on track. It can get very exhausting as we try to pull ourselves out of this digital black hole of weaving needs and wants like threads. We are not sure where one starts and the other ends.

This is not to say that everything that is not a dire need must be immediately eliminated. There may be legitimate wants that may benefit you or your family, but it helps to have some mental compartments to work with. You may even find value in saying out loud, "I/We are going to ____ (insert want) for 5 minutes," and then turn on a dedicated timer (not on the smartphone!) to ensure that you stick to this limit and not get distracted. It may help to refer back to the decision making principles, tools, and specific recommendations already discussed in this book to help you make balanced parenting choices.

Digital Parenting Principle #3: Nurture a Love for Literature

In the digital age of endless distractions, superficial thinking, and reduced attention spans, books are a family's best friends. Whether it is for education or healthy amusement, if we are not making books a regular part of our family life, then we are missing a source of critically important bonding and family fun time as well as alone time for us and our children. Books can be incorporated into family life in several ways.

With younger children, parents can find a way to enjoy reading aloud with them, ideally every day, for example at bedtime or after school. This is a great way to bond with children and have fun by using different voices for the different characters in the story. Let children get the message that you would rather be with them than doing anything else.

With older children, you can hold book clubs where the whole family takes turns to choose a book, read it and discuss it together. Through books, a number of issues can be discussed sensitively and with different perspectives.

In either case, parents can become proactive curators of books that will resonate with you and your children. There exists a plentiful supply of books that instil positive values through fiction and non-fiction, Islamic and mainstream.

Digital Parenting Principle #4: Nurture a Love of Nature

Part of the allure of digital technologies is having an easy escape hatch from the discomfort, challenges, and negative emotions of the real world. When we bump into the built-in limits of the real world, we can jump into a digital world with seemingly limitless options. When we despair against the inconvenience of physically travelling somewhere, we can click into an experience that is being produced across the world. When we get bored with this world, we can enter a virtual all-you-can-eat buffet of titillation.

As technology, computing power, and artificial intelligence progress, we are heading towards a techno utopia in which companies will promise us the ability to be in a virtual world in which we can be anyone and do anything we please. All this intoxicating ability in this virtual quasi-paradise will take us and our children away from the real world. As people around us continue to be seduced by this virtual reality, we must remind ourselves that the "imperfections" of this world, when looked at deeply, are not actually flaws but features.

The constraints, problems, and inconveniences of this world were designed by its Maker for us to realise something. We don't get resourcefulness without constraints. We don't get innovative solutions without problems. We don't get stronger without the inconveniences of having to move our physical body. We don't tame our *nafs* without pushing its buttons. We don't realise our utter need for the Divine without seeing our weakness.

All of this is to say that the anti-venom of this virtual, quasi-paradisiacal world we are approaching is the natural world. When we open our eyes to read the Divine messages in the natural world, we realise that it truly cannot be improved upon by a virtual one. As parents, we need to give our children the tools and love to find spiritual solace in nature so that they can fall in love with it and its Creator.

Digital Parenting Principle #5: Build on Current, Healthy Real-world Interests

As adults, we go through periods in which we are intensely interested in certain topics or activities. We may not even understand why something has grabbed us, but most of us know the feeling. It feels like an exciting wave. Our children are no different. The question is distinguishing which waves we allow to pass, and which waves we try to surf.

From past experience, we know that most of humanity will be caught up in the digital tsunami. But that does not have to be the fate of our families. We have already mentioned literature and nature as two healthy and enjoyable alternatives, but you may find that your children come up with other healthy alternatives of their own.

There are so many spiritually, mentally and physically healthy, real-world interests that parents and children can explore together, such as sports or a craft or community work. In order to guide parents as to which activities would be worthwhile pursuing, here are three factors to consider:

1. Success breeds pleasure and so it is worth considering is the child good enough at the activity to gain long term enjoyment from it? What classes and coaching is available for them? Are they interested enough to sustain this activity?
2. Will it offer some useful, real-world skills? Are the skills transferable to other real-world interests? For example, will they learn resilience, discipline, punctuality, service, teamwork or patience?
3. Could it be used as a platform to build strong family bonds? Can we engage in this activity together to further build our relationship?

Even if an activity does not optimise all of the above criteria, we can still bear in mind the benefit of our child being away from a screen.

Digital Parenting Principle #6: Prefer Learning Tools That Allow Focus

A key part of parenting is ensuring that our children receive an education that will serve the ultimate purpose of pleasing the Divine. As discussed earlier, multitasking can feel productive, but is, in fact, highly unproductive. In the same way, digital learning activities can feel "educational", but be exactly the opposite. While some useful digital learning tools exist, preference should be given to materials and learning activities that are low-tech and highly interactive.

For example, while most children will need to eventually learn how to efficiently type on a keyboard, the art of handwriting activates and strengthens parts of the brain that typing does not. While reading on an internet-enabled digital device may be highly convenient, physical books offer an experience that encourages more imagination, deep reflection and mastery. While flashy and elaborate educational games seem like they are bringing education into the 21st century, they simply cannot compete with an interested parent with a white board and set of flash cards.[103]

Overall, parents and teachers should ask themselves: do the learning activities my child is engaging in lead to more distraction, device addiction, and superficial thinking, or do they encourage focus, curiosity, and deep critical thinking?

Of course, this requires us parents take an active part in our children's development and be proactive in suggesting activities. This may look different from family to family, but fully outsourcing this function to other people and digital environments comes with many perils, the least of which is children simply do not learn the critical skills to help them navigate the real world.

Digital Parenting Principle #7: Become a Student of Parenting and Behaviour Change

As a conscientious parent in the modern age, the deck is stacked against us. Many of us cannot practically live without these devices that are designed by thousands of multi-disciplinary experts making thousands of decisions to optimise one thing: monetisable human attention.

Not all fields are equally useful for this aim. The usual suspects of hardware and software engineering would not surprise us. What may

---

103 Kimberly Berens, *Blind Spots*, 2020

surprise us however is the investment of the thousands of experts in behavioural psychology.

Many readers of this book will have gone through over a dozen years of schooling. In order to have college degrees and professional qualifications, it is not unusual to have gone through nearly 20 years of education to procure a livelihood or career.

However, when we are blessed with a responsibility as large as raising another human being, we tend not to have the same mindset. Perhaps we do not appreciate the enormity of the task in front of us or we underestimate how difficult it is. We may have seen previous generations parent without apparently putting in so much effort.

The questions to ask ourselves of our parenting endeavours is: what goals and values do I have as a parent for raising the trust that Allah blessed me with? What are my expectations for the characteristics of a well-raised child? Were the previous generations up against a multi-billion-dollar industry based on surveillance capitalism that capitalises on the manipulation of human desire? Did they live in a world with as much spiritual and moral decay and entropy as we do today?

Conversely, there have never been so many valuable faith-based resources that give Muslim parents general and specific strategies to bring the best out of children.[104] As Muslim parents, if we are not willing to invest the time and effort to educate ourselves on faith-based parenting in the modern age, then we are doing ourselves and our children a disservice.

---

104 Glenn Latham, *Power of Positive Parenting*, 1994

Preparing Your Family to Thrive

We are trying to give our children a versatile set of skills to prepare them to be successful Muslim adults in a world which they will have to contend with. We may have some glimpses of that world now, based on the direction in which we are headed, but we simply cannot predict all the specific details. However, we can give our children the tools to spiritually thrive. As parents, we need to learn to prioritise what our children learn and not simply follow the status quo. Learning to recite, memorise and understand the Qur'an is of the earliest of learning goals. Learning the Arabic language will open for them a wider scope of learning the rich Islamic tradition. We can work to cultivate in them a love of Allah, His Messenger, the righteous, and the Hereafter. We should teach them the essentials of Islam in terms of beliefs, external actions, as well as internal character. These are means that will lead to a beautiful, noble and happy life in this world and the next, and thus must be prioritised from the very first years of their life.

Additionally, learning basic practical skills which are often missing in the modern schooling system are also key learning goals. Camping, sewing, farming, woodwork, archery, horseback riding, are examples of life-long skills that have practical applications, and that help children disconnect from screens and re-connect with the natural world. We cannot ignore the above learning essentials or place them in a secondary position to other subjects/skills they may learn.

If we think that the digital tsunami previously described can't get any more towering, then we may be underestimating the pace of change. Adding in a few elements of artificial intelligence (generalised and specific), quantum computing, metaverses, brain-computer interfaces, and so on, we may find out that we are just at the beginning of this wave, and our children's and grandchildren's worlds may get exponentially more complex.

When Prophet Nuh ﷺ begged his son to join him on the Ark, his son replied, "I will go to the mountains, they will save me from the water." Prophet Nuh ﷺ said, "Today there will be no salvation from the Divine command, except on whom He has mercy" (Qur'an 11:43). A wave then separated them forever.

There are many lessons we can extract from that brief interaction, but most relevant for this discussion is that of a parent who understood the world he lived in and was willing to both prepare a refuge and put his trust in the Divine. As parents, we must do our part, because the time to build our family's ship is now.

> *when we keep ourselves occupied with healthy living, we simply don't have the time to be on our devices*

7

Healthy Living in the Digital Age

Our physical body has a direct relationship with our brain and our soul. A weaker body will result in a weaker mind. A weaker mind is more susceptible to be overcome by the digital addictions that we are seeking to release ourselves from.

So this book would not be complete without a discussion of how we can look after our body in combination with our heart and mind and soul. Bodies fed on unhealthy foods will result in a weak mind that is more susceptible to be overcome by the digital addictions that wait to ensnare us. In addition, when we keep ourselves occupied with healthy living, we simply don't have the time to be on our devices and we become more self aware of what is nourishing for us. Taking care of our bodies is not simply a worldly matter, but rather a religious obligation as well. Our Prophet ﷺ taught us that, "Your body has a right over you" (Bukhari). And when someone asked him who is the best of people, he replied, "He whose life is long and his deeds are good" (Tirmidhi). Taking care of our physical health is a means to a longer and more fulfilling life.

Many of our mental, physical, and spiritual ailments are due to the poor quality of food we eat, the large quantities we consume and our sedentary lifestyles. Making the changes towards healthy living is not difficult, and comes down to a few basic principles. People are often confused with regards to nutrition; what to eat, what not to eat, what is healthy, what is harmful. It is beyond the remit of this book to give specific nutritional advice but the following general advice will be of benefit to us all.

1. Avoid added sugar. Added sugar has many negative effects on our health, is the source of many inflammatory and chronic illnesses, and negatively impacts our brain function.[105] Sugar is also very addictive, which is why food manufacturers put it in almost everything. Choose foods that do not have added sugar, and avoid adding sugar to foods you prepare at home.

2. Avoid vegetable oils. Vegetable oils include things like corn oil, canola oil, and cottonseed oil. They were never used historically until modern times, and have been found to be pro-

---

[105] Abu Muni Al Sha'ar, Mirza A. Ashraf, *Food Between Curse and Cure*, 2020

inflammatory, effecting the brain and the other organs of the body in numerous ways.[106] One should stick to using olive oil, butter, or ghee.

3. Avoid refined carbohydrates. Refined carbohydrates are a significant source of disease in the modern world. Refined carbohydrates are carbohydrates that have been processed into a fine powder, ie made into flour. The flour is then made into various foods that are commonly eaten such as bread, pasta, cakes, cookies, etc. Carbohydrates processed and consumed in this manner have an extremely high glycemic index, and cause an immediate glucose and insulin spike in the body, which has multiple deleterious effects over time.[107]

4. Minimise consumption of meat. Animal proteins are an important aspect of our diet, but when consumed excessively negatively impact our health. One should aim to consume meat 1-2 times a week at most.

5. Avoid fried foods. Fried foods are high in AGEs, advanced glycation end-products, which have been associated with inflammation and dementia.[108] Unfortunately, most fried foods have also been fried in vegetable oils, further compounding their negative effects.

6. In each 24 hour period, give your body at least a 12 hour period without food. Just as the body needs periods of activity and periods of sleep/rest, it also needs periods of satiety and periods of hunger. We should make sure to always keep a period of at least 12 hours in the day without food/snacks. So if we finished dinner at 9pm last night, we should refrain from eating until after 9am the next morning. These daily periods without food are essential for hormonal processes in the body to help heal and repair the body.

---

106 Ibid
107 Ibid
108 Michael Greger, *How Not to Die*, 2015

7. Eat to feel satisfied, but do not fill your stomach. The Prophet ﷺ said, "No man fills a container worse than his stomach. A few morsels that keep his back upright are sufficient for him. If he has to, then he should keep one-third for food, one-third for drink and one-third for his breathing" (Tirmidhi).

8. Eat foods that strengthen the brain. In general, we should try to eat carbohydrates that are of lower glycaemic index, fruits and vegetables, sources of lean protein, and healthy fats. Healthy fats come from olive oil, nuts, avocados, salmon, and sardines just to name a few.

9. Eat real food. We should try to eat healthy nutritious foods made from real ingredients. If we see a food product with tens of ingredients, some of which are not recognisable, then it is likely that that is not good for you. It is a good habit to eat mostly home cooked food, which will have much more *barakah* (blessing) as well.

Aside from what we put into our bodies is the religious obligation to keep our bodies active. Our sedentary lifestyles have caused many chronic diseases of the modern age, and weakened us mentally and spiritually, making us more susceptible to the onslaught of digital devices.

Corporations much prefer our children to grow up glued to a couch while on their digital devices as opposed to playing outside. We sleep at night laying in our beds, only to get up to sit in a car to take us to school or work, where we remain sitting for eight hours. We then drive back sitting in our cars again, to get back home to sit again at the dinner table, followed by sitting in front of the TV or computer. We end the day getting back into bed, only to repeat it all for decades. Our bodies were not meant for this. Our souls were not meant for this.

In the past, daily life itself was physically demanding, and it kept people physically and mentally healthy. Whether having to ride a horse, or walk to the well and carry two buckets of water back home, or walk to the market, strenuous activity was naturally built into life. In the modern area of ease and luxury, these elements are no longer intrinsically there, and so we need to supplement them. We need to stay active at least a few times a week, with some type of exercise, whether it be walking, running, hiking, biking, gardening or strength training. With just a few pieces of equipment at home, or even none at all, there is no reason we cannot stay strong and fit. We do not have be fully paid up members of a gym to be healthy. In fact, it is probably spiritually more uplifting to be in nature. Keeping busy in this way also helps us reduce our screen time naturally.

> *relying upon Allah, worshipping and obeying Him, abstaining from what He has prohibited, strengthening our connection with Him*

8

The Greatest Means

The Strongest Means in the Age of Digital Deception: Our Spiritual Armour

Although some of what we mention in this chapter has been discussed at some level throughout the book, we felt that this topic deserved its own chapter given its central importance. We have discussed many practical means in this second part of the book, on how to make better choices in our relationship with the digital world. However, in addition to all these means we cannot emphasise enough that the strongest means we have at our disposal are those that are purely Divine in origin.

These are the spiritual means of relying upon Allah, worshipping and obeying Him, abstaining from what He has prohibited, strengthening our connection with Him, and seeking the Prophetic protections from deception and evil, from the lure of the world and the whispers of *shaytān*, and ultimately from the desires of our base *nafs*.

These means are intended to fortify our spiritual heart against the negative energies it is exposed to, voluntarily or involuntarily and are our greatest weapons against the onslaught of digital deception. Gradually and regularly incorporating these spiritual practices into our lives is *the only real way* we have to be able to safely traverse the modern day challenges we face. The deceptions will only increase, and without being fortified spiritually, we will likely become another statistic consumed by the digital world. The digital tsunami that will come crashing will leave no one unscathed, but only those who have their roots firmly grounded spiritually will remain standing, by the permission of Allah.

We often relegate these spiritual resources as an afterthought or a backup after we rush to other more worldly means as a first resort to solve our problems. Perhaps this is a product of the materialism that has found strong roots, even in the hearts of believers. The reality is, these spiritual acts are also a means, and the strongest of means. We must realise that everything happens by the Will and Decree of Allah. He is ultimately in control. So the most direct means to change our situation is to connect with and implore the One Who is truly in control. Taking worldly means, which are beneficial and warranted in the Divine scale, while neglecting these most essential spiritual means is a recipe for serious disappointment.

The Prophet ﷺ advised Ibn Abbas, "I shall teach you some great words. Be mindful of Allah, He will protect you. Be mindful of Allah, and you will find Him in front of you. If you ask, then ask Allah; and if you seek help, then seek help from Allah. And know that if all the people gathered to benefit you, they will not be able to benefit you except that which Allah had written for you; and if all of them gathered to harm you, they will not be able to harm you with anything other than that which Allah had written for you. The pens have been lifted and the ink has dried" (Tirmidhi).

Through this hadith, the Prophet ﷺ is teaching us the realities of *imān* (faith) and *tahwīd* (Oneness of Allah). Contingent created things have no power or ability in themselves, and all power and might is with Allah. He is the only One Who brings benefit, and the only One Who can ward off harm. The scholars say regarding the Prophet's instruction: "If you ask, then ask Allah; and if you seek help, then seek help from Allah," that this does not mean we do not seek help or ask others. Rather, we must see that they are simply a means Allah created. The scholars say what this instruction from the Prophet ﷺ means is to ask Allah first, seek help from Allah first, and then seek worldly means, knowing that the outcome is with Allah. This is true reliance on Allah.

Unlike some other also positive worldly means that have been discussed in this book, these practices are not bound by time. They will *always* be relevant, essential and effective until Allah inherits this world and what lies upon it. Our goal is developing a spiritual armour that will, by Allah's grace, make us much more prepared to navigate the age of digital deception.

Du'ā': Weapon of the Believer

One of the most essential and effective means, yet so simple and easy to access, is that of supplication or *du'ā'*. Unfortunately, this is often neglected. What makes it so incredible is the realities that it imbues in our hearts. Through *du'ā'*, we absolve ourselves of any ability to take positive action or ward off harm, and instead acknowledge our utter neediness for Allah, completely surrendering to His infinite ability. While we seek the means, we do so, not with our own contingent abilities, but with His infinite independent power and might. What deception can stand in the way of such power? To call upon the Divine with complete humility, focus, certainty and consistency is an essential means for safe passage through the trials of our time.

Salāh: Connection with the Divine

Salāh, as the root of the word indicates, is our connection with the Divine. Severing that connection would be the greatest loss to say the least. We must first ensure that we offer our obligatory prayers and do our best to never be neglectful of them. We must then work to improve the quality of our *salāh,* until it becomes as it was for the Prophet ﷺ when he ﷺ said, "The refreshing coolness of my eyes (i.e. my comfort) has been provided in *salāh.*" The stronger our *salāh,* the greater the means it will be to ward off harm.

The Prophet ﷺ said, "Verily Allah says…. 'My servant does not draw near to Me with anything more beloved to Me than the religious duties I have obligated upon him. And My servant continues to draw near to me with supererogatory works until I love him. When I love him, I am his hearing with which he hears, and his sight with which he sees, and his hand with which he strikes, and his foot with which he walks. Were he to ask of Me, I would surely give to him; and were he to seek refuge with Me, I would surely grant him refuge'" (Bukhari). What deception will stand in the way of the one who hears, sees and walks in this world with the Love and Light of the Divine?

Remembrance: In the Presence of the Divine

There are numerous verses and Prophetic sayings instructing us to be in a constant state of Divine remembrance, such as his ﷺ saying, "Let not your tongue cease to be moist with the remembrance of Allah" (Tirmidhi).

In a general sense, all acts of worship are a form of remembrance. More specifically there are essential forms of *dhikr* we should introduce as part of our spiritual routine.

The Qur'an is also called the *dhikr* (Quran 15:9) and indeed the best words to repeat are those revealed by Allah Himself. The Prophet ﷺ said, "God who is blessed and exalted says, 'To him who is occupied with the Qur'an from asking of me I will give him the best of what I give to those who ask.' The superiority of God's words over all other words is like God's superiority over His creatures" (Tirmidhi). Thus having a regular daily habit of recitation of the Qur'an is essential as it is a means of shielding against the negative onslaughts of our modern world.

In addition to the Qur'an, the Messenger ﷺ taught us a treasure of remembrances to recite in the morning and evening as a means of spiritual fortification. Take for example the following remembrance:

بِسْمِ اللهِ الَّذِي لَا يَضُرُّ مَعَ اسْمِهِ شَيْءٌ فِي الْأَرْضِ وَلَا فِي السَّمَاءِ وَهُوَ السَّمِيعُ الْعَلِيمُ

Bismillāhi ladhī lā yaḍurru ma'asmihī shay'un fil 'ardi wa lā fī samā'i wa huwa samee 'ul 'alīm

In the name of Allah, with Whose Name nothing harms in the earth nor in the heavens, and He is the All-Hearing, the All-Knowing (Tirmidhi)

The Messenger ﷺ informed us that whoever reads these words 3 times in the morning and evening will not be harmed by anything, and will not be afflicted by a sudden calamity.

Additionally the recitation of part of or all of *Surat Al-Kahf* is very important as a means of protection from deception of the end of times, as our Messenger ﷺ instructed (Tirmidhi).

When we become accustomed to reciting these (and other words of remembrance) in the morning and evening, and we reflect on their meaning, it becomes a source of incredible spiritual energy and protection, by the grace of Allah.

Repentance and Seeking Forgiveness: Door of Divine Bounty

One of the essential means of Allah's endless bounty and of purifying our heart is often returning to Allah in repentance (*tawbah*) and seeking forgiveness (*istighfār*). Allah says in the Qur'an, "Ask your Sustainer to forgive you your sins – for, verily, He is All-Forgiving! He will shower upon you heavenly blessings abundant, and will aid you with worldly goods and children, and will bestow upon you gardens, and bestow upon you running waters" (Qur'an 17:10-12). It is also a means of protection (Qur'an 8:33), a means of Allah's Love (Qur'an 2:222), and a means of success (Qur'an 24:31). The Prophet ﷺ said, "If anyone continually asks pardon, God will appoint for them a way out of every distress, a relief from every anxiety, and will provide for them from where they cannot imagine" (Abu Dawud).

***

These elements are just a few but essential spiritual practices that will help us in this age of digital deception.

THE ROAD
AHEAD

> *We have never had such an array of solutions to human problems and challenges.*

Final Thoughts
Trial of our times

Our Beloved Prophet ﷺ warned us of the signs of the end times and the greatest trials which will befall humanity. Confusion and deception will be widespread.

We live in the most advanced technological age in human history. We have never had fingertip access to so much information. We have never been able to fulfil so many tasks from the comfort of our homes – indeed from the palms of our hand. We have never had such an array of solutions to human problems and challenges.

Yet what price are we paying for this "advancement"?

There is no aspect of our lives that has remained untouched by this technological onslaught. Our brains have been reconfigured into addiction, anxiety, depression and insomnia. Our hearts are spiritually devoid from over consumption of mindless or harmful content. Our relationships with our families are suffering as we each sit in our own virtual worlds. Our community ties are weakened.

We have become sitting receptacles of data for corporations that gather it to extract more money from us, to manipulate us into spending money to fulfil our baseless desires, to socially engineer our thoughts, to create a surveillance economy.

We live in a dangerous world of virtual reality where truth and falsehood have become difficult to distinguish. And this virtual world is all in the hands of an ill intentioned few who manipulate and deceive billions of people across the globe for their own means.

The Last Generation

We now stand at a precipice. We are the last generation who will likely remember an age where smartphones, social media platforms, messaging apps, video games and the internet didn't exist. We lived through a time when life went on without the need for virtual digital experiences. We are the last generation that can likely show and separate the truly beneficial from the unnecessary and harmful. We are the last generation that has a before and after snapshot to compare. If we truly are the last generation before the Age of Digital Deception, then what is our calling? What is our role? What is our struggle and sacrifice?

Happily, significant numbers of people from all over the world and all walks of life are starting to realise that there is cause for concern.

Entrepreneurs, managers, software developers, youth groups, concerned parents, academics, are all realising the realities outlined in this book. They are making better choices to bring about a better life.

They are proactively taking steps to limit, and sometimes eliminate, access to certain programs or gadgets. Even many of the makers of these programs and gadgets, the experts if you will, after seeing what they have produced and their harmful effects, have distanced themselves and their children from their use.[109]

So that is our role. That is our duty. That is our struggle. To ourselves, our children, our families, our community, and to humanity. To push back against these digital deceptions and to ensure our actions don't inadvertently draw others into being further addicted to these technologies and platforms.

When we continue to casually use these platforms, when we casually buy them for our children to use, when we use them even for calling people to good, we validate them, we become part of the tangled problem. Now that we have an awareness of the issues and the challenges ahead, can we consciously and knowingly let others suffer as a result?

Action Emanating from a Serene Heart

The believer uses both their spiritual and physical faculties to be aware of the nature of the problem, to identify the best means of tackling it and then to act to protect themselves, their families, the believers, and humanity at large.

Often, even if we are able to do the first two steps of truly being aware and identifying the best solutions, we lack the resolve to follow through with actions that we know will benefit us and those around us.

109 Jeff Orlowski, *The Social Dilemma*, 2020

This lack of resolve is a spiritual pandemic that we ask Allah to lift from us as well as all believers. Our Beloved Messenger ﷺ commands us: "Do not be incapacitated (due to challenges you will face)" (Muslim).

We must approach the difficulty with a heart at peace, knowing that this is all under the Will and Destiny of Allah. We must not worry who will win. Allah is ultimately in control of the situation, and will deliver in peace and safety those who strive to be people of *taqwa and tawakkul* (Allah-conciousness and reliance). When a man asked the Prophet ﷺ when will the Final Hour be, the Prophet ﷺ replied, "What have *you* prepared for it?" (Bukhari).

So, we are not called to random worry. We are not called to useless complaining. We are called to purify our hearts and take action. "So make provision for yourselves, for the best provision is *taqwa*" (Quran 2:197). It's time we have *taqwa* with these devices and platforms.

It is out of Allah's Mercy and Divine Care and Support for the believers that He always provides alternatives for us. We have mentioned many of these alternatives when navigating the digital world.

These are most impactful when combined with a holistic approach of healthy living and spiritual means. Even if we have to engage with the digital world at some level, we need to turn to Allah and beseech Him to not allow our hearts to be attached to it.

Our role is to be a sincere seeker, and take positive steps in our life, fulfill our obligations to the best of our ability, abstain from the impermissible, and take action against the challenges around us and within us. We leave the rest to the Grace of Allah.

"The one who aims will arrive."

While decreasing our usage of these digital programs and gadgets, we need to fill our lives and the lives of our families, with more nourishing alternatives. Only through "filling the cup" of our lives with good will we be able to dilute, and eventually remove, the harmful.

If we spend our time in the company of our families, if we attend to our parents and children, if we explore nature, read books, serve our communities, partake in hobbies, reconnect deeply with Allah, we simply won't have the time or inclination to live in a narrow virtual world once we have experienced the joys of the real world.

Every generation of this Ummah has struggled with its unique challenges, and within every generation have been those who rose to those challenges with intelligence, moral beauty, and courage. From the brutality of the crusades rose the chivalry of Salahuddin Al-Ayyubi. From the superficiality of mechanical worship rose the poetry of Rumi. From a world of racial injustice and mental colonialism rose the piercing truth of Malcolm X.

If this is one of the most defining struggles of our time, then the question must be asked: who amongst us will have what it takes to see its reality? Who amongst us will have the moral beauty to swim against the current? Who amongst us will have the courage to free themselves and others from the invisible shackles that we put on ourselves? Who amongst us will rise?

We ask Allah by His infinite Mercy and subtle Beauty to show us truth as truth and enable us to follow it. We ask Him to show us falsehood as falsehood and enable us to stay away from it. All good can only come from Him and we truly cannot do anything without Him.

We ask Allah to accept this work as being sincerely for Him. We ask Him by His grace to make it for us and not against us on the Day when we all will return to Him. *Allah knows best and success is only through Him.*

About Sagetree Foundation

Sagetree Foundation seeks to revive the light and wisdom of the Prophets and sages, to help people navigate the darknesses and confusions that are ever so prevalent today. While the enemies of humanity are many, the light is one. The Light of God and His Messenger, which is the source of light for the sages, the righteous, and all those who travel their path.

About The Authors

Dr. Amir Abdelzaher is an instructor at Al-Madina Institute's Suhba Seminary. He obtained his Ph.D. from the University of Miami in Environmental Engineering and taught at several universities before deciding to focus his energies on education for Muslim children. He has founded multiple Islamic schools, and has been studying and teaching the Islamic sciences for nearly two decades. He currently resides in Istanbul with family.

Arfan Qureshi is Senior Director of Talent & Organizational Development at the Campbell Soup Company, where he is responsible for the talent strategy, design, and execution. He has previously held senior learning, leadership, and organizational development roles at Comcast and the Hershey Company. Arfan has consulted internationally in the Middle East and Africa. He is also co-founder of Sagetree Foundation. He obtained his master's degree in Change of Management Coaching and Consulting from a joint program between Oxford University's Said Business School as well as HEC Paris's School of Business. He also holds a master's degree in Social and Personality Psychology from Michigan State University. His passion is parenting, child rearing, education, and Islamic spirituality. He resides in New Jersey with his wife and two children.

Dr. Ahmed Howeedy is a Family Medicine physician in Boca Raton, Florida, where he serves as Chief Medical Officer for FHE Health, a Substance Use and Mental Health facility treating psychiatric and addiction disorders. He also serves as a Medical Review Officer and USCIS Civil Surgeon. Dr. Howeedy obtained his medical degree from the University of South Florida in Tampa, and his undergraduate degree in Microbiology and Immunology from the University of Miami. During his medical studies he pursued his studies in the Islamic sciences. Dr. Howeedy is also Managing Director for Sagetree Foundation. He is currently completing his degree in Islamic Jurisprudence from Jamiat Al-Ulum Islamiyya al Alamiyya in Amman, Jordan. He currently resides in Boca Raton with his family, serving as board member, teacher, and youth instructor at the Islamic Center of Boca Raton.